GARDEN
MAGIC

Inspired Garden Design

GARDEN MAGIC

Inspired Garden Design

Gisela Keil • Gary Rogers

HORTICULTURE
BOOKS
CINCINNATI, OHIO

A DAVID & CHARLES BOOK

David & Charles is a subsidiary of F+W (UK) Ltd., an F+W Publications Inc. company

First published in the US in 2004 ISBN 1-55870-736-0 paperback

Originally published under the title *Garten-Glück*
© 2002 by Deutsche Verlags-Anstalt GmbH, Stuttgart München

Distributed in North America by Horticulture Books, an imprint of F+W Publications, Inc.
4700 East Galbraith Road, Cincinnati, OH 45236
1-800-289-0963

A catalogue record for this book is available from the British Library.

Printed in China by SNP Leefung
for David & Charles
Brunel House   Newton Abbot   Devon

Desk Editor: Sarah Martin
Production Controller: Roger Lane

Visit our website at www.davidandcharles.co.uk

David & Charles books are available from all good bookshops; alternatively you can contact
our Orderline on (0)1626 334555 or write to us at FREEPOST EX2110, David & Charles Direct,
Newton Abbot, TQ12 4ZZ (no stamp required UK mainland).

Contents

QUALITY
GARDEN
LIVING

The perfect answer to the stresses and pressures

of modern living is undoubtedly the garden.

Whether for company or solitary pleasure, patios,

bowers, pavilions and seating areas in the garden,

or by the water's edge, help increase our

enjoyment of the natural and calming surroundings

of our home environment.

Patios For All Seasons

◁ Pages 6-7:

So refined. This elegant, shady, terraced patio combines individuality and a formal layout. The snug seating area is created by dividing the larger area with interlocking beds, and evergreens, for example box and azaleas, providing a solid framework; while pale pink petunias provide a splash of seasonal colour. The stylish clinker-brick herringbone flooring is set off by attractive ornamental garden furniture.

Patios allow you to experience the seasons with all your senses without leaving the comfort of your own home. Here you can listen to the blackbird's springtime call, inhale the balmy scents of the summer garden or savour the culinary plenty of the autumn harvest together with your friends. Even in winter, the patio adds value, if well designed, when viewed for itself, from the window of your home, or for taking in the view of the garden from the patio itself when its structure affords some protection from the elements.

Regardless of their size or style, patios should always be able to fulfil a dual function: as independent spaces, green refuges which satisfy our need for leisure or company, and also as an aesthetic and architectural link between house and garden. This of course means that the patio's design must combine ideas from both house and garden in a harmonious manner.

You can establish the extent to which this successful combination is already present in your own home by asking yourself the following questions:

Does the patio provide a pleasing view of the garden?
A patio's recreational value is also based on the aesthetic appeal of its surroundings. So the most important aspects are those such as the view, access to the garden and privacy.

Observed from the garden, does the patio fit in harmoniously between the garden and the house?
Viewing the patio from a different angle helps you to determine whether it complements the house in style, colour and design, facilitating a natural fusion of garden greenery and domestic architecture. This perspective also allows you to establish whether house, patio and garden are in pleasing proportion.

Your aim is for a patio with a soothing ambience, that provides a comfortable yet stylish setting for you to relax in the fresh air.

Left:
Convivial company. A patio is the perfect place to play host to your guests. The backdrop formed by the climbing rose ('New Dawn') on its wooden trellis affords visitors a tantalizing glimpse of the verdant garden beyond, while the white Victorian-style iron bench invites them to sit back and savour summer pleasures.

Right:
A recipe for the good life. Patios allow you to indulge in the open air, enhancing your living area from spring through to autumn by providing room for the whole family or a tranquil sanctuary where you can take a quiet break. Adjoining the house, they absorb heat from its walls in spring and autumn, and this makes them cosier and more comfortable. At the same time, this patio's low surrounding walls adjoining the garden elevate it and thus counter the colder and damp air at ground level, especially during cool evenings.

Patio and garden harmony

The first step in any patio design must be a consideration of the surroundings. If house and garden lie on the same level, the patio must be built on a slight gradient (at least two per cent higher than the level of the garden), in order to allow rainwater to drain off.

Detached houses with large gardens can accommodate larger patios with additional and more elaborate leisure features. In addition to the seating and barbecue area considered necessary for the average-sized patio, a large 'canvas' can provide for a play area for children or even a swimming pool and sunbathing area. The garden section on to which the patio opens should also be planned with the patio in mind, with prominent plants like trees or shrubs placed at varying intervals to lend the area structure, depth and variety. The bigger the garden, the higher these plants should be. One to two individual varieties, chosen for their attractive leaves, blooms and/or autumn colouring, should be placed near the patio. These arrest the gaze, framing the patio as if it were a picture, and give a sense of security as well as allowing you to experience the seasonal changes of nature. Shrubs, in

Salon with a view. From this spacious patio, the garden resembles a magnificent parkland scene. Under the canopy formed by the pergola, entwined with climbing plants, the patio has an air of intimacy. Yet, the staggered positioning of the trees lends depth to the vista, helps direct the eye across the scene and encourages the cosseted patio-dweller to leave, and explore the garden delights beyond.

Minimalist and meditative. This terraced house with a patio stretching the entire width of the building is transformed by using a modern, formal design which plays with space and light. The lighting effects and reflective furnishings give the illusion of distance, of extra space on the raised platform, which provides room for conviviality and meditation alike. The eye-catching gravel beds, the evergreen box and the tall screening bamboos ensure that the view out on to the garden remains attractive all year round.

particular evergreens, can improve the appearance of unattractive surroundings and prove extremely effective screening devices for particularly distracting eye-sores. However, in more rural settings it is advisable to leave some areas free, preserving the view from the garden out on to the open countryside.

In the case of terraced houses, the patio usually stretches the entire width of the house, normally shielded on each side by a screen, allowing you to view a small strip of garden. Spaces like these can appear bigger if planted with mid-height plants to form a backdrop. Smaller shrubs, long-stemmed plants or trellises of climbing plants are ideal because they don't take up much space. Taller shrubs, however, especially those with a large spread or bold presence, make small gardens appear box-like, making them seem even smaller.

If building on steep plots of land, it is better to create two different levels linked by steps. Hillside patios feel more intimate if enclosed by a low retaining walled border, built up to about seat height. This raised part of the patio requires the most protection from the wind, with robust shrubs or other screens that will also provide extra privacy. Its free upper section, backing directly on to the hillside, can house a magnificent, fragrant display of flowers at nose and eye level.

Smooth transitions

The patio should not appear out of place when observed from the garden but rather give the impression of providing a harmonious setting for enjoying the views. This is achieved through carefully creating attractive border areas, bearing in mind all the different garden plants and colour schemes that could be used during the design process. Low embankments can be planted with climbing plants, while perennials or roses from the flower beds bordering the patio look more effective if encouraged to spread out and encroach upon the patio itself. Larger, more obtrusive seats can look cosier and more inviting with luxuriant, bushy plants placed in close proximity to them. Smaller patios seem more generous if they merge unevenly with the garden, allowing the plants to spill out over the edges.

Traditional backdrop. This rather wild yet bewitching patio, on which lady's mantle (Alchemilla mollis) has been encouraged to grow liberally, forms a charming contrast to the historic building's architectural austerity and the formal gardens. From the patio, visitors can enjoy the vista of the interlocking bed of golden-green box, a classic sundial and the shaped, green-yellow holly bushes.

Elegant alliance. The house and patio with its ornamental balustrade, wooden flooring and wicker furniture blend in an alliance of elegant white. The striped cushions and cheerful fuchsia-filled hanging baskets add a welcome touch of colour, enhanced by the climbing plants entwined around the pillars. The subtly scattered plants keep space free for social activities, while still continuing the garden theme. The more substantial design ensures comfort and protection from the elements.

An attractive patio ambience

The design of a patio is determined by its size. About 10–15sq m (108–161sq ft) is adequate for a seating or eating area. However, if you need to provide for many guests – perhaps for holding parties – you should allow 30–50sq m (323–538sq ft). On the principle that 'less is more', small patios often appear bigger thanks to fewer materials and colours as well as harmonious contours. Patios which jut out, on the other hand, have their appearance improved if subdivided using specific features which provide comfort and yet structure – whatever the season – such as hearths, ornamental ponds, stone fountains, raised beds or little islands of plants.

The choice of surface and design of the flooring is crucial for both large and small patios. It should match the house and be echoed in paths and seating, especially in smaller gardens. The choice includes a large variety of paving slabs or flagstones (natural stone or concrete), in addition to clinker bricks, wooden boards or panels which can be laid in a variety of patterns and combining different materials. It is of course possible to introduce variety into larger areas by creating mosaics with frost-resistant glazed tiles, pebbles and many other materials. Yet it is wise to bear in mind that

Mediterranean flair. The French-style wrought-iron furniture looks great on the reddish sandstone slabs, a striking presence, yet not dominating the space. The large parasol completes the Mediterranean feel and, hopefully, will be needed for long, hot summer days of leisure.

Naturally interwoven. Pergolas
provide shade for seating areas
and a degree of privacy. Anchored
in the flower bed and fixed to the
wall of the house, they take up
very little space on the patio. This
pergola's roof of solid, round
wooden beams entwined with
climbing roses creates pleasing
dappled shade. The visitor can sit
underneath and enjoy the beautiful
fragrance of the roses. The wooden
floor decking is appropriate for the
small-scale surface area and
makes the patio appear wider.
The practical blue folding seats
echo the colour of the door and
window frames.

uneven surfaces and wide gaps can be a nuisance when it
comes to placing furniture and moving around.

The patio's success as an intimate and secluded refuge
providing for quality leisure time requires the use of some
form of screening. Walls, hedges, wicker screens, reed
matting, palisades and trellises picturesquely interwoven with
climbing plants and erected on each side of the patio
provide some protection from the elements and a degree
of privacy. Roof coverings such as awnings, parasols or
pergolas afford welcome shade and privacy from above,
making the space below appear more attractive, with
pleasing patterns of light and shade.

Unstinting elegance. The awning,
reflecting the bright white of house,
plants and furniture, provides shade
at the touch of a button and
harmoniously complements the
magnificent stone patio. Larger
areas are more suited to striking
floor patterns, such as these
rectangular, natural stone flags
bordered with granite cobblestones.

Below:

An eye-catching patio border. Make rigid contours a thing of the past! Introduce fragrant roses, grasses or budding perennials from the flower bed on to your patio, breaking up the austere edges around the patio with magnificent pots.

Break it up. *Large patios appear more intimate when divided up with plants in attractive, aesthetically pleasing tubs, troughs or pots. While most patio and pot plants only provide colour until autumn, evergreen woody shrubs such as box give the patio structure and interest throughout the year.*

Ideas for stylish potted gardens

Transform your patio into a fragrant sea of colour by planting a potpourri of pots and tubs with a selection of today's huge choice of patio plants, bulbs and summer flowers, perennials, herbs and shrubs.

Some plants are perfectly suited to the smallest patios, for example both annual and perennial climbing plants that take up little horizontal space, but whose long climbing stems can cover entire walls, pergolas and trellises; and hanging baskets, which also require no floor space and whose flowering contents guarantee abundant colour all summer long. Long-stemmed plants or trailing plants cascading down from pillars and other supports won't hinder those using the patio if varieties chosen are not too vigorous or thorny. When

On the edge. The top of the patio's brick border edging can be used for plants and displays. Here, varieties of Sedum and Saxifraga are arranged in cast-iron pots with stones and large seashells. Climbing or trailing plants look good here too.

Potted gardens. Place the flowerpots against the wall on stands at different heights and plant them with both bushy and trailing plants. An alternative would be to make a hanging garden using baskets.

A study in green. This patio is so much more inviting with the wall adorned by hanging baskets and climbing plants. It is also enriched by the diverse variety of potted plants that frame the seating area. The consistent colour tones present in the clinker-brick flooring, brick wall, wooden furniture and clay pots increase the harmonious nature of the entire ensemble.

choosing flowering plants, it is important to consider the scent and shape of the blossoms as well as the range of colours. A harmonious effect is produced if colours from the garden are echoed in the house or accompanying décor. When creating single displays, choose long-stemmed plants, elegant-structured shrubs or resplendent pot plants to guarantee an impressive show. However, as a general rule, it is better to group plants together to add to their appeal. Experiment with themed arrangements which match the patio's style, based on a Mediterranean or herb garden, a display using scented plants, a kitchen garden, a garden eating area or a colour-coordinated garden (using only white or blue, for example). Another idea is to create a subtle arrangement using many different types of one plant variety. There is a wide range of attractive and innovative small water features on the market that can also be used to add interest to the patio. Choose containers and frost-resistant garden accessories which match house and patio in style, colour and material. Finally, select your plants carefully. However, beguiling blossoms may not be enough to realize the full potential of the patio. A welcoming atmosphere is often only perfected through appropriate accessories, carefully arranged to their best advantage.

Enduring structures. A patio can be enhanced not just by a display of plants but also by charming artefacts, properly framed, such as these attractive clay pots on a brick plinth. It looks better to display these at different heights. Those used for winter displays should be frost resistant and, whatever the season, not in the line of traffic, so as to avoid breakages.

Scenic Garden Seating

Away from the patio, seating areas in different sections of the garden can provide a whole new set of impressions and experiences. Here, seated in the midst of nature, worlds away from the daily grind, you can relax and observe the house and garden from totally different perspectives. As you savour the rich delights of blooming shrubs, fragrant roses and colourful flowers you can relax, wind down, observe and enjoy all the sights and sounds of the garden's natural inhabitants.

Seating for all occasions

Just as a house has many rooms fulfilling different functions, garden seating areas can fulfil the different requirements of the various family members, in harmony with nature. Anyone whose patio is used predominantly for entertaining guests will appreciate an intimate, secluded seat where they can read and, perhaps, daydream. On the other hand, spacious barbecue areas in the garden, far away from the house and the neighbours, are ideal for uninterrupted celebrations. On hot summer days, a cool green spot with a welcome source of shade fits the bill. Alternatively, the sun-worshippers among us can enjoy eating breakfast in east-facing areas and watching the sun go down in the west. As the different parts of any garden provide their own particular seasonal highlights, putting the seating in such locations allows you to experience all the magic of the seasons.

The precise nature of the seating depends on its intended function. Large social gatherings require groups of seats or walled seating. If privacy, seclusion and time alone with nature is desired, a small area with a bench, chair or stone seat will suffice.

These points need consideration before the design process is begun, as the position, size and layout of the seating will be determined by what you will be using it for – and how often – as well as by the size and style of the garden itself.

A bench with a view. There can be few more peaceful and relaxing places to sit than in the dappled, swaying shadow of a broad-leaved tree. A circular bench such as this one is ideal for quiet or convivial get-togethers, affording a varied panoramic view of the garden as it changes with the seasons. Painting wooden benches a distinctive white effectively catches the eye, while leaving them in their natural state ensures they blend in with their surroundings.

Right page:
A cosy nook. Secluded seating away from the house tempts you into the green richness of the garden and allows you to enjoy in comfort the beautiful, fragrant plant world. If the seats are going to be in frequent use, it is advisable to lay some form of attractive, frost-resistant flooring, which will be another pretty garden feature in itself.

Seasonal seating. Where better to enjoy the last rays of the autumn sun than amid the beauty of an ornamental grass arrangement? Eulalia (Miscanthus sinensis), fountain grass (Pennisetum alopecuroides) and stonecrop (Sedum telephium) are at their absolute best at this time. Planting the area with bulbs creates a second festival of blossoms in spring, tempting you to sit down and simply enjoy.

Location and design

Your personal preferences, combined with the style of your garden, will determine whether the garden seating is designed to blend in inconspicuously or attract the eye. When the grounds are close to nature or freely laid out, the seating can remain hidden, yet must provide a pleasant prospect and a certain 'je ne sais quoi' like special blossoms or fragrances. On the other hand, seating areas in formal gardens play an essential role in their architectural design, often functioning as important reference points in the middle or at the end of vistas and pathways, or even in front of topiary hedges. England's formal gardens provide a wealth of classic role models, with their world-famous benches, which are not only functional but also beautifully crafted works of art in their own right.

It is a good idea to secure seating which is in frequent use. Mobile seating, on the other hand, offers flexibility, allowing you to move as the fancy takes you. The surface on which the seating is placed should be frost-resistant, non-slip, and, above all, stable; not made of soft sand or wood chippings, and without any wide gaps for the chair legs to fall through. White floor surfaces are unsuitable in sunny spots, reflecting the sun's rays and generating an unpleasant glare. As was the case with the patio, the material used for the flooring, as well as its

Magic circle. Sit snugly in this sunken circle and savour the gorgeous rhododendron blooms. Over time, the Chinese wisteria (Wisteria sinensis) will entwine itself around the steel supports, transforming the spot into a fragrant bower.

Room for the senses. This fragrant seating area, with its backdrop of roses, purple lavender (Lavandula angustifolia) and the tangy scent of the white feverfew (Tanacetum parthenium), exudes an aromatic bouquet to stimulate all the senses.

colour and the way you lay it out, should not clash with that of the house. Certainly, pathways leading to the area should be coordinated with the seating. Bordering smaller areas with more finely patterned materials makes the whole thing seem much more in proportion.

Seating areas are, by and large, rectangular or round, with round spaces often seeming more dominant. If the area is supposed to be a focal point of the garden, its shape can be precisely planned. Being garden architecture, demarcated areas and pathways such as these give the garden structure, so the design and position of the seating should be carefully considered.

Garden seating on raised or lowered ground is an innovative alternative. Raised areas provide you with a good view but need to be well surrounded by taller plants to avoid giving occupants the feeling of being on show. Lowered seating areas also make the garden seem larger, but low-lying spots are potential frost hazards for plants as the heavier, colder air tends to collect in them.

Design tips: plants and furniture

It is a strong and natural human instinct to seek protection from potential threats from the rear. Providing such protection, privacy and shelter against the elements is

Staged setting. Seating areas can be used for dramatic purposes, even in the most casually designed gardens. A path winding its way in and out of the willows steers the gaze towards the group of seats positioned in the background, before which a 'still life' of urns and amphoras has been skilfully created.

therefore a must for any seating area. Placing seats in front of walls, hedges or tall shrubs helps achieve a feeling of security. In formal gardens, benches can often be found encircled by a semicircular green garland of topiary hedges. If space is at a premium, a similar background can be created with elegant latticed trellises or pergolas entwined with climbing plants, such as climbing scented roses, honeysuckle or clematis. Attractive seating areas, although requiring some protection from the back and sides, also need pretty views from the front. Pathways should present house and garden from a new angle, maybe with a striking frame created by placing arches, elegantly trimmed shrubs or specially chosen perennials in the foreground or centrally, as points of reference. That said, you should also be able to enjoy viewing your garden close up. As individual flowers and leaves can be best appreciated at close quarters, feel free to

A shaded spot by your miniature garden. A shady garden nook can be enhanced by a water garden in tubs and other small attractive features. Ornamental plantain lilies (Hosta), box, miniature privet bushes and strawberries planted in various receptacles all play their part well, as do the Japanese hops (Humulus japonicus) near the sculpture by the trellis. Completing the picture, water soldiers (Stratiotes aloides), water lettuce (Pistia stratiotes) and water lilies (Nymphaea hybrids) bob about with floating candles in barrels and tubs.

Sitting at the edge of the garden. With just a little imagination you can transform a remote spot into an enchanting refuge. Pink and delicate violet clematis wreathes the connecting wall while at the foot of the shade-giving tree is a magical blanket of plantain lilies (Hosta), perennial false spiraea (Astilbe) and a beautiful rose.

put plants right next to the seating area. The area can be further enhanced by garden accessories, plants in tubs and high-quality, weather-resistant furniture.

Small areas retain the illusion of space with slender, cast-iron furniture, while for more classic gardens solid, old-fashioned wooden or stone benches really do look the part. Shaded spots or darker yew or ivy hedges can be brightened up with white furniture. This colour can contrast with neighbouring blossoms or harmonize attractively as required. Variously, the choice of material and style can lend the area a Mediterranean flair, the restrained air of an English formal garden, an Eastern feel, a general rustic or romantic ambience – whatever you fancy.

Stone seating as garden artistry

Seating as garden artistry. Situating benches on grass or amid flowery scents invites you to savour heavenly aromas. This is an old tradition which inspired the designer of this garden to invest in this fine stone bench. It was planted with a variety of Roman chamomile, 'Treneague' (Chamaemelum nobile), which compensates for its lack of blossom by forming a strongly scented mossy carpet.

Antique-looking benches of recent manufacture, carved from natural stone are better considered atmospheric garden décor, rather than as practical, comfortable seating, but can be positioned to good effect. Nowadays, the most beautiful replicas are available in frost-resistant or natural stone, and if placed in damp and shady spots they will soon 'grow' a picturesque coat of moss and lichen and very soon look like originals.

Movable seats

These encourage spontaneous enjoyment of seasonal attractions, for example sitting under the budding branches of an ornamental cherry tree in spring or amid a flowery early summer meadow. Transportable furniture which does not necessarily have to be weather-resistant is the perfect solution here.

❶ For daydreamers. The smooth swaying of a hammock is wonderfully relaxing. All you need are two tall trees the right distance apart.

❷ Grassy seating area. Suitable only for occasional use, for example during celebrations on the lawn when guests have been invited and the patio would otherwise be overcrowded.

❸ A bench in the shade of the house. A perfect retreat where you can enjoy a quick cup of tea, chop the vegetables for lunch or read the paper.

❹ Romance. An elegant white bench nestling between roses and clematis.

❺ Blossomy retreat. From the prospect of this blue cast-iron seat, rose-lovers can enjoy the luxuriant white blossoms of the rambling rose.

❻ Nostalgia. There is a quaint, old-fashioned feel to this scene, with comfortable wicker chairs inviting you to take a siesta in the shade of the apple tree.

Idyllic Water Features

If you include water in your garden design, ensure you can enjoy it up close and in comfort. For this reason, seating and water are inseparable partners. Sitting by the water's edge, enjoying the water's refreshing coolness in summer, stimulates all our senses. The different levels of light and the diverse vegetation of the changing seasons are reflected in the water's sparkling surface, and its splashing and lapping noises help you relax and unwind.

Moreover, water is host to many plants and animals which you can observe at close quarters. You can also place water directly on the patio in basins, wells and fountains or position it next to the patio as a link with the garden. Alternatively, water can be a separate feature, perhaps combined with seating in a secluded spot.

Water on the patio

Water features can be used to strikingly divide up large patios. Ornamental ponds filled with water, whether round, rectangular, square or freestyle, always seem generously sized when the patio's flooring extends right up to the edges of the pond.

Even small patios can be animated by the charm of water. Natural stone troughs, barrels and other, modern receptacles can be chosen to match the style and materials of any patio. And there is now available a wide and inexpensive range of charming, small, portable water features that work well even in a limited space.

Water can also be directed to trickle through antiquated or modern gargoyles, which take up little space and can be fixed on the side of the house or patio, with the water dropping down into metal or natural stone basins built into the wall.

Another individual touch could be the addition of water channels installed along the patio's edges. Fountains are especially attractive, as much an audial as a visual delight.

Reflective treat. The light, as it changes throughout the day and from season to season, the surrounding plant life and the weather (sun, wind and rain) all dapple the water's reflective surface with ever-changing shades and patterns. Creating a seating area directly above a pond makes for an exceptionally peaceful setting. Wooden decking which eventually weathers to give an attractive silver effect is especially suited to a natural garden design.

Right page:
The magic of water. This seating area, tastefully arranged on a circular stone surface and overlooking a pond, is perfect for friendly get-togethers and has views of both water and garden. The robust seating, on the solid-looking, opaque stone pavers, contrasts effectively with the fluid, reflective surface of the water. A miniature bubbling fountain is sufficient to enliven the pond's surface while water lily leaves hold the promise of a transient, blossomy splendour. Ice plants (Sedum spectabile) growing over both areas, link seating and pond in summer and then in autumn with first green, then magnificent burgundy, foliage.

Water borders

Patios bordered or encircled by ponds, pools or water courses should always be built above the water to provide the best viewing platform. There are various ways of creating the divide between patio and water. The patio's edge can be designed to run straight or curved; it can be built as a rectangular or semicircular platform or on staggered, sweeping slabs reaching out into the water. In the gardens of narrow terraced houses, a popular choice is to install ponds the entire width of the garden and then to give access over them by way of stepping stones or footbridges.

In gardens like these, it is better not to mark out the edge of the pond with rigid lines. Natural ponds can end in a curving bank, whereas a subtle diagonal or staggered effect at the edge looks good in ornamental pools.

When installing ornamental ponds with fountains, ensure that the water jet is not so strong that a gust of wind will blow it as far as the seating area. Sodden seating or, worse still, a sudden soaking for the guests, is hardly conducive to a water idyll!

Round and blue. The different elements in this themed modern design were planned to blend together. The two main design features, namely 'blue' and 'round', can be seen in the seating and in the pond. Although these are built on three different levels, they succeed in forming an integrated whole. The blue-sprayed bricks impressively encircling the pond set the colour tone. The aquatic plants in their fibreglass basins and turquoise bowls accentuate the colour scheme.

Lying by the pool. Making space to lie down by the edge of a swimming pool, screened at the side and from behind by means of careful planting (as in this example, with shrubs and tall miscanthus) or wooden cabins, is a recipe for pure pleasure. In hot, sunny regions, it is usual to tile the pool light blue or turquoise, which makes the water appear even cooler and more refreshing.

Sitting and lying by the water

Water features – particularly larger installations – are special areas of the garden and it is wise to plan the seating well in advance. Even a few large, suitably shaped boulders can double as seating, giving a really natural and appealing look when placed by a meandering stream. Hillside gardens provide a natural setting for water steps or waterfalls, and seats can be placed at the foot of the cascades for a wonderful view of the flowing water.

A circular watery stage. This construction, with steps that can be used for both lying and sitting on, immediately brings an amphitheatre to mind. The strictly formal architecture merges seating and pool and requires little space. The water falls like a melodic curtain into the pool, making its surface sparkle before being swallowed up again by the circular funnel and the entire cycle begins anew.

Bowers, Pavilions and Summer Houses

In contrast to less elaborate and portable seating, bowers, pavilions and summer houses are generally more substantial, intimate refuges providing extra comfort, privacy and security. They stand as bold architectural structures in the midst of their natural surroundings. They first featured in Italian renaissance gardens and 17th century English formal gardens. During the 18th century they pervaded landscaped gardens, their ornamental style moulded by the contemporary rococo influences. They were sometimes surrounded by the most exotic flowers obtainable and began to acquire a romantic aura as a secret trysting place for lovers during the course of the 19th century. While members of the middle class tended to rendezvous in garden bowers, the nobility met in pavilions or in the then newly invented greenhouses or conservatories. Today, with rigid social divisions largely a thing of the past, it is the cost of such structures that now matters for most people. Whether selecting contemporary models or indulging a taste for the exotic extravagance of centuries past, you will have to consider the design of your garden and where you wish to position the seating architecture. If it is to be situated close to the house and patio, it should match them stylistically, but if it is situated a little way off, it can be allowed to leave its own imaginative mark on a particular area of the garden.

Picturesque feature. Attractive pavilions placed at the edge of the garden or in secluded corners provide unexpected surprises, especially when they become a feature in themselves through the addition of an ornate bench or exotically oriental roof. Surrounding shrubs and leafy plants ensure they integrate with nature and guarantee visitors privacy as well as protecting them from the elements.

Bowers

These intimate garden structures are often romantic conceptions, taking the form of benches, overarched with greenery, whose roof and walls are moulded from climbing plants or shrubs. Surrounded by plants, you can sit in the bower's atmospheric dappled shade where the only disadvantage is the lack of complete protection from the rain! Bowers gain their shape from the plants themselves or their trellis supports. You can therefore let your imagination run wild, whether you prefer artistic, vintage, white-painted trellises or a

Right:
Just the place for a tête-à-tête. Ornamental edgings, lattices and black cast-iron struts form an elegant octagonal bower. The ivy thrives in the shade and has been allowed to run wild over the bower, giving this intimate nook an airy yet cosy feel.

Below, top:
Glass palace. Built podium-style on a slight slope, this modern pavilion has wonderful views, especially of the tree foliage!

Below, bottom:
Verdant architecture. This beechwood bower with bird bath has been formally designed as an architectural feature.

bold, asymmetrical steel framework. The trellised bower can be rounded off nicely by fragrant climbing plants such as climbing roses, honeysuckle *(Lonicera)*, wisteria *(Wisteria)* or old-fashioned sweet pea *(Lathyrus)*.

However, climbing plants are not always necessary, and if a really natural look is sought or more of a children's den is the objective, then dense round bowers can be woven from cut willow or hazelwood canes which swiftly take root after planting and put forth new growth. Alternatively, bowers using trees are well suited to park-like or formal gardens. These can be created by planting trees in a semicircle or open square and weaving branches of an appropriate height together before placing a bench in the space beneath. It is even possible to transform solitary trees into bowers provided that, when fully grown, their leaves and branches spread wide yet also hang down, rather like an umbrella; try using the camperdown elm *(Ulmus glabra* 'Camperdownii'), weeping ash *(Fraxinus excelsior* 'Pendula'), Young's weeping birch *(Betula pendula* 'Youngii') and Yoshino cherry *(Prunus yedoensis* 'Shidare-yoshino').

Pavilions

In contrast to bowers, pavilions are open or at least half open at the sides with a closed, often very extravagantly worked roof. They can have a rounded, quadrilateral or multi-angled

Below, centre:
Bower in an alcove. The white bench, bird house, pillars and doves transform this roofed seating area into the perfect setting for romantic encounters. Tastefully chosen long-stemmed plants on either side complete the picture.

Below, right:
Rosy pavilion. Open trellised windows encourage climbing roses to colonize this octagonal pavilion, reached by a typically formal, straight path, whose entrance is clearly marked by two topiary box hedges.

Magical tree house. These structures can be erected in solid, mature trees, enticing you to spend days up in the branches. This example is a cross between a summer house and a belvedere, encircled by climbing roses and shrubs, with a potted garden spreading out on the stairs and balcony.

shape with room for a group of seats, and an elaborately fashioned framework for their walls is the norm. This sophisticated style is based on a long tradition of ornamental architecture. Pavilions were first found in baroque and renaissance gardens. In 19th century formal gardens, it was fashionable to place them in the centre or at the end of a path as a striking feature. Built high on slopes, cliffs and even in trees during the 18th century, they were meant to both provide and constitute the view. This meant they often took the fashionable form of temples, pagodas, South Sea huts or rustic retreats while at the same time they functioned as belvederes, commanding a fine view. However, in less structured gardens, pavilions set back in secluded corners can be charmingly romantic and provide new views of the garden. As protected, cosy seating areas, today's offerings made of wood, metal, steel tubing and glass are just as popular as their predecessors.

Summer houses

This type of garden structure is completely enclosed and provides a comfortable retreat. Wide doors and windows are a necessity to ensure a pleasant view of the garden. Like pavilions, they blend in with the garden greenery through the use of climbing plants, with the addition of shrubs and perennials as borders and frontage.

Blending Architecture and Nature

If gardens are allowed to outgrow their limits, they not only appear larger but also look less contrived, more natural, and altogether more appealing. Here, the magic word is 'integration', which helps prevent unnatural breaks in a harmonious whole.

• External transitions. Gardens seem considerably larger if their extremities or boundaries are disguised by swathes of plants, making them as inconspicuous as possible. In town gardens, this is most effectively achieved through creating a screen with evergreen shrubs or climbing plants such as ivy or honeysuckle (*Lonicera henryi*), which wreathe walls in colour even in wintertime. In countryside gardens, however, it would be a pity to conceal the beautiful surroundings outside the garden; far better to 'bring' them in, to make them an integral part of the garden borders, by creating, for example, paths between shrubberies and encouraging the gaze to roam beyond the garden's edge into the natural world beyond.

• Internal transitions. The garden's influence should also be present on the house and garden architecture in order to avoid clashing lines and contours. This is of particular importance in town gardens surrounded by other people's houses and gardens, all expressing the diverse tastes of their owners. Planting the area colourfully, but judiciously, helps buildings blend into the vegetation, and the plants growing in close proximity or actually encroaching on to buildings will again, by blurring boundaries, seem to increase the size of the garden.

Harmonizing plants

• Shrubs. A broad-leaved tree, planted at the side of the house, contrasts visually with the building, which in turn appears sheltered rather than isolated. Ornamental shrubs, planted near the house, perform a similar function. Examples of these are the witch hazel (*Hamamelis* hybrids), fragrant

Climbing in company. The clinging power of ivy and Virginia creeper (Parthenocissus quinquefolia) makes conquering walls no problem at all for these tenacious plants. The less tightly clinging stems of the Virginia creeper often hang down attractively in long trailing cascades. The greenery undergoes a striking transformation in autumn when the Virginia creeper glows a flaming red next to its evergreen ivy partner.

Right:
A fluid progression. The flower bed and Virginia creeper (Parthenocissus tricuspidata 'Veitchii') scaling the front of the house merge so seamlessly here that the garden almost overflows into the house. In the bed itself, evergreen shrubs such as yew, pine, heather and rhododendron seem to be migrating towards the house, shrouding it snugly in a coat of green even in wintertime, while in summer the dwarf spiraea 'Little Princess' (Spiraea japonica) provides a touch of pink. Strikingly overgrown architecture like this is enchanting, but is not essential in order to unify house and garden.

viburnum (*Viburnum farreri*) and snowy mespilus (*Amelanchier lamarckii*), which captivate with their early blooms and the splendour of their autumn colouring. Other beautiful candidates include lilac (*Syringa*), magnolia (*Magnoliaceae*), hydrangea (*Hydrangeaceae*), buddleia (*Buddleja*) and stem roses.

Climbing shrubs for livening up your house walls

Climbing rose grows to 8m (26ft) on lattice, many scented varieties

Clematis grows to 10m (33ft) on lattice, some scented varieties

Honeysuckle grows to 5m (16ft) on lattice, sweet-smelling

Wisteria grows to 10m (33ft) on lattice, scented

Dutchman's pipe grows to 10m (33ft) on lattice, in sun or shade

Silver lace vine grows to 15m (50ft) on lattice, in sun or shade

Virginia creeper grows to 15m (50ft), magnificent autumn colouring, clinging

Climbing hydrangea grows to 7m (23ft), scented, clinging, thrives in shade

Ivy grows to 20m (65ft), evergreen, clinging, thrives in shade

---

• Climbing plants. These help the garden to take the house by storm, they frame canopies and doors, entwine themselves around balconies and balustrades and transform patio pergolas into green canopies. It is crucial to choose plants correctly here. Some require trellising in order to give the front of the house visual structure. Others can weave their way effortlessly up the house wall through sheer clinging power. Evergreen climbing shrubs are suited to sunny and partially shaded spots. Their blooms are pretty but they do tend to shed leaves easily which can mean a lot of additional work. There is also an attractive assortment of annual climbing plants to choose from.

• Espalier fruit. Those wishing to combine the attractive with the functional can plant south-facing walls with pears, apricots or peaches, trained up decorative trellises.

• Flowery combinations. Flower beds that extend to or run alongside the house or line the patio are another alternative. Perennials, summer blooms and roses join evergreen shrubs (box, for example) that will look good even in winter. Finding room for a narrow bed of tall flowers along the side of the house is rarely a problem, suitable varieties including the delphinium (*Delphinium* hybrids), lupin (*Lupinuspolyphyllus* hybrids) and hollyhock (*Althaea rosea*).

Potpourri. Several different ways of decorating a wall are used here: the delicate pink climbing roses and pink and violet petunias stretch upwards and are met halfway by the yellow turrets of the mullein (Verbascum).

Colour design

Ensuring that colours for climbing plants or flowers on the house match those in the garden creates a feeling of consistency. Beautiful effects can be created using combinations of different plants, or mixing plants which bloom at different times.

Rosy splendour. A blooming medley of fragrant bedding, shrub and climbing roses is assembled around this doorway, creating a traditional cottage atmosphere.

DESIGNING WITH SHAPE, COLOUR AND LIGHT

Arranging plants according to their size and

the shape and colour of their foliage and blooms

is an important element of garden design.

This is the key to bringing space into a small

garden – order into a rambling space. Adding

tasteful artificial lighting will then allow you to

enjoy your garden by night as well as by day.

Successful Planting Schemes

◁ Pages 38-39:

Perennial fireworks: The yellow spiky blooms of the foxtail lily (Eremurus hybrids) form a striking contrast, in both shape and colour, with the purplish-blue lavender (Lavandula angustifolia) and its little waves of downy blossom. They are combined with the cream, red and pink bed roses in concert with the golden yellow fan-like blossoms of the Atlas fescue (Festuca mairei).

Static. Trimmed into square blocks, box radiates the same restful effect as in its spherical form. As a green focal point it arrests the gaze, as illustrated in this intriguing chessboard pattern.

A plant's appearance and power of expression are influenced by the different types of growth, leaves and blossoms. Tall herbaceous perennials, grasses, herbs or attractive shrubs are especially effective and can stand alone as isolated garden features. However, it is usual to arrange plants together, whether in large or small groups. Successful plant arrangements where shape and colour are emphasized are based around four basic principles which apply to all plant varieties:

• Contrast. Combining contrasting plant forms and colours makes garden designs more interesting, exciting and effective. For example, round-shaped plants are well complemented by column-like or conical types; large, broad-leaved plants by those with filigreed, finely feathered foliage; and a sea of tiny blossoms by large blooms dotted here and there. This is why groups of plants containing individual types of widely differing form and height, like roses or herbs, need a steady framework of lavender or box, a stabilizing element (such as a statue or bird bath) or the unified backdrop of a topiary hedge. It is important to ensure that the contrasting pairs are not equal in impact.

• Rhythm. Repeating particular arrangements of colours and shapes at regular intervals in large beds and borders and also in the garden as a whole gives the area a certain equilibrium.

• Simplicity. It is never wise to play all your cards at once when dealing with shape and colour, particularly when planning smaller gardens. Less is always more and the result is always more harmonious.

• Timing. While evergreen shrubs are an enduring garden presence, flowers are only at their colourful best during certain times of year. This means taking the blooming season into account when working with plants.

Right:
An imposing show. The tall purple moor grass (Molinia caerulea ssp. arundinacea 'Skyrace'), which has decorative autumn colouring, erupts majestically in fan-like golden fountains. It is combined with the elegant, grey hair grass (Deschampsia), whose rather nondescript panicles unfurl from early summer onwards and which can reach 2m (6¹/₂ft) tall. It enlivens every bed with its dominating structure.

Striking contrast. Two tree trunks, rising up like mighty vertical pillars, form a striking contrast to the gently curving horizontal lawn and ivy bed below. The contrast is tempered by the green which holds sway over the whole scene, particularly the ivy which acts as a link between the horizontal and vertical features.

Trees and shrubs

Trees and shrubs are the garden's tallest plants and most powerful design components. Over the years they help to create an enduring structure within the garden and a feeling of space and depth. Their appearance is also important as it can influence the garden's atmosphere, depending on the rigidity or fluidity of their contours.

Tall shrubs

Tall trees make the area seem smaller, making them unsuitable for smaller gardens.

Spherical, conical and column-shaped plant forms, especially those of ever-green leafy shrubs or conifers, appear dignified, calm and solemn in their uniformity. While spherical forms draw you in, eye-catching cones and columns have a more dynamic effect as a result of their vertical structure. Spherically trimmed topiary trees, spheres, cones and columns are popular in formal

A pondside play on form. The five topiary box spheres add a touch of the formal to this free-style garden. Their apparently arbitrary arrangement means they fit in perfectly, toning in with the overhanging blue-green shoots of the blue Atlas cedar (Cedrus atlantica) at the edge of the pond as well as with the bushy shrubs and the thrusting stems of the great reedmace (Typha latifolia).

Romantic fancy. Shrubs and trees with spectacular, uneven growth stand out in solitary arrangements. That said, intertwining climbing plants are always effective, softening the harsher contours of tree trunks and branches. Here, the ivory climbing rose 'New Dawn', its petals tinged with pink, works its magic on an old apple tree.

gardens. They can be planted in rows to form an avenue or can flank paths, beds, house entrances or benches. They work well and also prove a worthy addition to more casual arrangements, providing the eye with a point of reference or a resting place in an otherwise busy-looking scene.

Shrubs and trees that have an unusual habit or whose branches grow upwards or outwards in a striking way – such as willow (*Salix matsudana* 'Tortuosa') or overhang like an umbrella always seem livelier or more elegant. However, the more mobile and fanciful the form, the more stable the surroundings and background need to be. Shrubs with overhanging growth look extremely impressive when planted on embankments or on the tops of walls with their magnificent cascading shoots tumbling over.

Colourful shapes. Shrubs and trees that overhang like an umbrella, such as the Japanese maple (Acer palmatum 'Dissectum'), appear striking when planted alone at the edge of a pond or on the lawn, their foliage providing brilliant autumn colour. These trees can also be pleasingly integrated by using round boulders which echo the shape of the top of the tree or shorter plants of similar growth.

Contrasting agendas. The yellow candles of the leopard plant (Ligularia 'The Rocket') and the juniper's bluish-green stanchions rise up dynamically, framing the wide funnel shape of the mountain fern (Thelypteris limbosperma). The leaves, too, play their part: the groundsel's thick, large, heart-shaped leaves confront the fern's light-green, doubly feathered fronds, which stand out splendidly against the solid blue-green of the juniper.

Working with herbaceous perennials

Because perennials vary in their foliage, flowers and general appearance, they lend themselves well to garden design in so many different ways.

• Foliage. Using plants with different types of foliage and planting them in increasing order of height will guarantee you attractive flower beds. It is advisable to plant beds set against walls, hedges or pergolas so that the perennials will grow up on one side only, whereas those in island beds can be encouraged to grow up on all sides, forming a central pyramid. Nevertheless, this increase in growth should not appear too abrupt, but should form curving contours to display the individual varieties to best effect. Grouping perennials imaginatively according to their form also works effectively. Upright, erect plants can be interspersed with branching or overhanging ones, while bushy or blanket perennials nestle at the bottom. It is, however, worth bearing

Top:

Successful combination. Arranging plants of the same colour tends to focus the attention on the shape and appearance of the leaves. The overhanging finely leaved bamboo forms a striking contrast to the large, but compact, decoratively veined chestnut leaves of the rodgersia (Rodgersia aesculifolia).

Middle:

Opposites attract. Leaves and vegetation can form charming contrasts with other natural elements such as stones, boulders and roots. Here, the broad stony ridge and narrow, sword-shaped leaves of the yellow flag iris (Iris pseudacorus) are poles apart.

Bottom:

Succinct shapes. Large, ornamental or useful accessories, such as bowls, sculptures or these clay planters containing sea kale, exercise a calming influence when set against the lively and colourful dahlias.

in mind that each type of perennial is subject to annual growth rhythms (budding, blooming and dying back) and therefore looks very different according to the season. If using relatively early-flowering varieties such as bleeding heart (*Dicentra spectabilis*), leopard's bane (*Doronicum*), globe flower (*Trollius europaeus*) or oriental poppy (*Papaver orientale*), which are quick to die back after blooming, remember that their albeit splendid floral displays can only be enjoyed on a short-term basis. The gaps which subsequently appear in the bed means that these varieties should never be planted in the foreground. However, there are many cultivars that enable the gardener to achieve a succession of blooms thereafter, right up until the autumn, using peonies (*Paeonia*), day lilies (*Hemerocallis*), plantain lilies (*Hosta*), bedding and rosette plants, grasses and ferns as well as tall bearded irises (*Iris barbata hybrids*) and Christmas roses (*Helleborus niger*).

• Although leaf forms are not as striking from afar as more bushy foliage, they do come into their own when viewed close up. Whether with large or small, round or straight, flat or finely feathered leaves, plants that do not flower but have attractive foliage can look stunning all the year round. Shady areas, normally unsuitable for flowering plants, can be charmingly decked out with leafy perennials of different shapes, sizes and surfaces. These may have a waxy sheen, be matt or felted and can be ribbed or veined in a variety of decorative ways. Shrubs and perennials with large sturdy leaves always stand out more effectively than those of the same size with more delicate foliage and are therefore better suited to larger gardens.

• Blooms. Although short-lived, individual blooms exhibit a rich variety of shapes (single, double, pendulous and so on) but it is really their colour which captivates. A harmonious balance is achieved using plants with small blooms more liberally, rather than the larger-bloomed varieties.

Working with Colour

◁ Pages 46-47:

Nature's own masterly design. Valid design principles can be discovered in miniature by those with an eye for detail. The heart-shaped leaves of water lilies stand out against the water's horizontal surface, also home to the invasive shoots of the common mare's tail (Hippuris vulgaris), which break the surface like little trees. The scene, redolent of a Monet painting, is made complete by the delicate red and yellow floral dabs of the water lilies (Nymphaea hybrids) and water fringe (Nymphoides peltata).

Like music, colours have the power to stir the soul and infuse every garden with a special atmosphere. It is therefore no surprise that their importance has always been recognized and used, as opposed to the consideration and deployment of shapes and forms. As an emotional and stylistic device, colour enables the gardener to create moods and effects and is predominantly linked to blossoms and leaves, whose transient natures often limit its power. Whereas painters merely have to keep their canvas in view as they work, the gardener must also work within the constraints of plants' life cycles and flowering times in order to produce what are often all-too-brief glorious pictures. On the other hand, this same transience allows the gardener to experiment with different shades and tones throughout the year.

Those wanting to discover the key to a world of colour are advised to go back to basics and begin with the primary colours (red, yellow and blue), which, when mixed, produce the secondary colours (orange, green and purple). All the above can be lightened with white (red to pink) or darkened with black (red to burgundy). However, the density, size and texture of the blossoms, the colours of neighbouring plants and the light itself can all modify a colour's particular effect. Here are some design tips:

• Combining bright colours results in striking contrasts, which can have a vivid, restless or aggressive effect.

• Softened, pastel tones go well together, have a calming and harmonious effect and make for charming garden displays.

• Warm colours such as yellow, red and orange penetrate the foreground and suggest proximity.

• Colder, more muted colours such as blue, purple and grey, blend into the background and give a feeling of distance.

• Continuous or large expanses of one or similar colours can be contrasted or livened up with dabs of another colour.

• Green, white, silver and grey are neutral colours which can help prevent colours clashing.

Left, below:

Colour as form. Colour can also structure, differentiate and subdivide. Violet crocuses herald the onset of spring, cutting a path through the golden yellow of the winter aconite (Eranthis hyemalis) and the accompanying snowdrops (Galanthus nivalis).

Right:

A lust for life. When you pair blue with orange and yellow with purple, they complement each other. The yellow and orange tones of the day lily (Hemerocallis) and yarrow (Achillea) complement the blue of the globe thistle (Echinops banaticus) and salva (Salvia nemorosa 'Blue Hill'). The little purply-red oval heads of the allium (Allium sphaerocephalum) tumble down in between.

Small gardens

In small gardens, less is more when it comes to colour. Using fewer colours or pastel tones is preferable to a riotous profusion of colours. Use blue, purple or grey blooms as a backdrop, and small spaces appear bigger.

White all summer long. Summer flowers such as cosmos (Cosmos bipinnatus) and the silver-leaved oxe-eye daisy (Leucanthemum vulgare) beguile onlookers right up until autumn.

An enduring green. The topiary spheres of box and privet combine with an ivy carpet to form an evergreen garden scene, while throughout the summer bushy lavender planted in pots conjures up a delicate scented vision of violet in front of the house.

Planting with one colour

Beds which use just one colour are perhaps rather unconventional. They might seem strange and contrived no matter which colour you choose – maybe because such uniformly coloured beds are at odds with the very diverse colours that abound in nature. In terms of design, it is important to note then that shape and form are accentuated by the lack of variation in colour, so these should be carefully chosen during the planning stage. Constructing single-colour flower beds therefore requires thorough knowledge of plants, which can be acquired through experimenting with small, seasonal arrangements or summer flower beds.

Colour combinations

Multicoloured beds can be created by combining plants with various colours of blooms and leaves, or even just using different-coloured foliage plants (yellowish green, burgundy, purplish green, silver and grey, as well as yellow or white variegated foliage, for example). Small gardens are particularly suited to a two-toned approach, which can

Fireworks during early and midsummer: lupins in many hues (from red through to purple) form the backdrop for the silky blossoms of the field poppy (Papaver rhoeas), which seem to dance on their thin stems.

produce a contrasting and spirited effect. Complementary contrasting colours, using a combination of one of the primary colours and a mixture of the other two (reddish green, bluish orange or yellowish purple), are normally very vivid.

The warm tones of similar colours such as orangey yellow or reddish yellow also suit this colour scheme. Classic English combinations include elegant yellowish white, pinkish silver (or grey) and purplish blue/yellowish green.

A harmonious three-toned effect can be achieved through adding white, silver or grey to the above pairings. The combinations of blue, yellow and white or grey, pink and

Colourful dissonance
Mixing secondary colours with the primary colour they are made from is often problematic. These shades lie on the cusp of the primary colour in question, and are as follows: red – yellowish red (orange) and purplish red (pink); yellow – yellowish green and orangey yellow; and blue – greenish blue and purplish blue.

Pretty blueprints for spring. When spring arrives, a carpet of blue will often appear at the foot of shrubs, like these examples: Siberian squill (Scilla sibirica), glory of the snow (Chionodoxa gigantea) and purplish-blue hyacinths (Hyacinthus orientalis hybrids). Displays using plants which, alas, bloom briefly like these, can be used for larger-scale plantings.

An autumnal repertoire of refreshing tones. Low-growing bushy aster with its bluish-green foliage (Aster dumosus hybrids), *tall Michaelmas daisies (Aster novi-belgii) and mountain aster (Aster amellus), whose beauty is already beginning to fade, bloom in thick clumps in front of delphiniums (Delphinium hybrids) whose second blooming is fast approaching and monkshood (Aconitum carmichaelii). Their blue stands out strikingly against the fading hydrangeas in the background.*

Right:
Classic colour trio: shades of blue, red and white are provided by light-blue delphiniums (Delphinium) and sweet-scented roses conjuring up a delightful summer scene.

dark purple are very striking. Combining the three primary colours, however, can often have unpleasantly 'loud' or clashing results.

A sub-range of colours can be formed from colours which are very similar in shade. They have a softening effect just like groupings of the same colour. These are formed by combining different shades of the same colour, which are then either lightened with white or darkened with black.

A series of warm colours. This rhododendron hedge seems to have leapt straight from a palette of primary colours, beginning in late spring with opulent purplish red and metamorphosing into carmine and scarlet before turning orange and yellow in the autumn.

Pages 54-55 ▷:
A medley of pastel blossoms. Here, the cottage garden works its artistic magic with a bright summer display. The large number of white blossoms softens the effect of more vigorous tones, creating an overall impression of delicacy. Cosmos (Cosmos bipinnatus) in white, pink and red, white ornamental tobacco (Nicotiana × sanderae), blue petunias (Petunia hybrids) and the little white heads of the feverfew (Tanacetum parthenium) floriferously engulf the sundial.

Playing with colour

Certain architectural components or garden accessories can be designed to tie in with plant shades, either repeating them or forming a deliberate contrast.

❶ Blue window shutters partner pink petunias framed in green.

❷ Bluish-purple wolf's bane with a blue glass bird.

❸ Blue metallic flower-bed borders help the dainty little orange blossoms to stand out.

❹ Blue ceramic pots, surrounded by green leafy plants, make up for the missing blossoms.

❺ Colourful harmony: red roses and a red sphere.

❻ Surface designs using muted colours and unusual surfaces (pebbles, houseleek (*Sempervivum*) and creeping thymus (*Thymus praecox arcticus*)).

❼ Three-dimensional chessboard pattern using moss and brilliant blue gravel.

Pale elegance

White, pastel-coloured blooms and silver and white-grey foliage can confer a delicate elegance and can be used to lighten up dark corners. When the daylight begins to dwindle, the flowers will come into their own. Shady areas under trees can be turned into an iridescent carpet of white foliage by using plantain lilies (*Hosta*), lungwort (*Pulmonaria*) and yellow archangel (*Angelica*).

Dancing, light-coloured patterns. The light blossomy veils of perennial false spiraea (Astilbe) and lady's mantle (Alchemilla mollis) brighten shaded shrubby spots even on the cloudiest of days.

Illuminating the Garden at Night

With the aid of atmospheric lighting, the garden can be transformed into a stage on which the colours and shapes of the plants and other elements of the garden are taken from the darkness and magically brought to life. The garden gains a new mood and dimension in the mysterious play of light and shade and can be used as an extended living area for quiet hours spent at ease under the stars or convivial summer nights. Lighting in the garden, used effectively and with a little imagination can both increase our enjoyment of the garden's features and amenities and also the amount of time we can actually spend there. It works to merge the house and garden harmoniously. It goes without saying that light makes both house and garden safer at night. But it would be a pity to limit the use of such an excellent design tool to the function of simple illumination.

Modern lighting methods and equipment can decorate and enhance the garden during the day as well as bring it into view at night. For example, there is an ever-growing range of innovative, solar-powered lighting effects that look attractive during the day when they are collecting and storing the sun's energy before radiating soft, gentle brightness with the onset of night. Designs include rocks and stepping stones in addition to the more traditional-looking lanterns.

Light sources and their uses

There are three main types of light which produce different effects depending on where they are positioned:
• Diffuse lights emit evenly scattered beams and form a visible focal point. The higher they are positioned for a downward beam or further away for an upward light, the larger the area they illuminate and the gentler the light and shade they produce. Because they are prominently positioned, choose an attractive design that will work well in the garden environment.
• Dimmed lights have the light source reduced somewhat

The old and the new. A grand old Venetian stone basin sits above a modern limestone channel. Underlying floodlighting results in impressive reliefs, while the illuminations are mirrored diffusely on the water's surface.

Right:
Light's magical power. A multitude of little lights entwined in the trellis roof and pavilion's interior create a 'temple' of light. An old parachute has been given new life as a voile curtain, filtering and softening the light and adding to the ethereal ambience.

or filtered, so as not to dazzle. Some models with adjustable fixings allow you to focus the beams as you wish.

Others are constructed so that the light can only be directed upwards or downwards, shedding light on a small area.

• Floodlights emit focused beams and are used to emphasize individual or groups of plants or objects. Spotlights are even more intensive, when illuminating smaller areas and details with precise cones of light. As floodlights do not come in a range of attractive designs and are placed away from the object they illuminate for the required effect, they can be concealed in the vegetation and thus avoid spoiling the garden's appearance during the day. Aim the beams upwards into the plants to create stunning and dramatic silhouettes. Leafy arches, spindly stems and eye-catching leaf forms will all become magical sculptures in the spotlight of the illuminations.

Top, left:

Mysterious world. Ponds and rocks are transformed into a fantasy world when illuminated. Floodlights embedded in the ground transform boulders into 'glowing' rock, while underwater floodlighting gives the pond's fountain a magical aura. The power centre with its colourful glass insets is mysteriously lit from within.

Bottom, left:

The shape of things to come. A central source of electric light placed at ground level between perennials provides the observer with a whole new perspective of the beauty and form of plants.

Top, right:

Light designs. The geometric cuboids housing white perspex lights blend perfectly with the white walls during the day and form a striking contrast with the perennials' various lively green shades. At night, their diffuse white light illuminates the scene, evoking a skyline of skyscrapers.

Creative lighting

Illuminated entrance areas offer greater safety and security and also deter unwanted visitors. Lanterns, wall-mounted lights or raised floodlights which turn on automatically when approached are very effective.

Steps, flights of stairs and pathways can be lined with dimmed lights on pillars or other raised supports to ensure safe night-time use. A creative touch can be added by illuminating individual flagstones in pathways or installing spotlights at ground level beside steps.

Patio and seating area lighting should never dazzle or dominate or the view of the garden will be lost. Using wall-mounted lights or indirect illumination with floodlights creates a softer, atmospheric light. Patios and seating areas look even more picturesque when decorated with table lanterns or old-fashioned oil lamps. Summer parties can be enhanced by festive

Bottom, right:

Highlights. The powdery blue of these frosted glass table lanterns adds a refined sparkle to the silvery purple plant arrangement, day and night. An odd number of lights is more harmonious than an even number.

Beaming beauty. The lights fitted to the pergola's framework are dimmed here from the front and succeed in emphasizing its delicate design. The rhododendron, lit from below, forms an island of light enhancing the whole spectacle.

chains of lights entwined in trees and shrubs, draped around pergolas decked with climbing plants or used to crown flower beds with bright festoons. Chinese lanterns, evoking childhood memories, and floating candles in bowls and tubs never lose their charm.

Ground-level floodlights produce a particularly dramatic effect, pushing leafy trees, shrubs, tall grasses or perennials into the limelight with the aid of upwardly focused beams. These are not directly fixed to stems and trunks but rather installed a short distance off, the light then being directed at the trunk, branches or crown.

Floodlights embedded in the earth can reveal different and hitherto unrecognized aspects of shrubs with the aid of their wide beams and are particularly suited to larger gardens, while mobile skewered spotlights are flexible and can be used in the smallest gardens, drawing attention to seasonal highlights – the first blooms appearing under shrubs or the magnificent autumn colouring of the shrubs themselves. Large, illuminated spherical sculptures and natural-looking stone lights, resembling boulders by day but bathing sections of the garden in soft light by night, and other modern

Design tips

• Gardens should not necessarily be lit evenly. In order to accentuate the charming play of light and dark, organize different sorts of islands of light for your garden.

• Placing lights in the foreground and background or centrally as points of reference creates a feeling of depth.

• Combine fixed and movable lights. Solar lights, whose collectors should face south where possible, make mains power unnecessary.

• When creating a new garden, ensure that enough conduit is laid down to provide you with electricity wherever needed.

designs, are effective garden features. The combination of light and water always has a magical romantic effect. Shrubs placed at the edge of the pond and illuminated from below are reflected in the water's surface along with other more romantic and captivating sources of light, such as the moon or stars.

Floating candles adrift amid the water lilies can lend ponds an air of mystery. Underwater floodlights can also create ingenious effects, particularly when focused on the water jets of fountains. As these can also illuminate unsightly things in the water, it is wise to light the surface of the water with slanting rays if the pond is full of algae.

Landscaped light. This lighting concept makes house and garden merge in a single illumination. Light provided by spotlights which vertically illuminate trees and shrubs causes them to be reflected in the water, creating visual counterpoints to the house. In contrast, the floodlights placed beneath the building send their beams skimming over the pond surface and garden, enhancing the overall effect.

DESIGNING AND DIVIDING

To create a visually stimulating design the garden

must be divided up using natural and architectural

devices. Experiment with patios, beds and borders

to break up the surface; arches, walls and trees

to add a vertical dimension.

Exploring Garden Design

◁ Pages 66-67:

Romantic space. Spatial design ideally involves fantasy and illusion. In this section of the garden, tall screening shrubs transform the area into a secluded, romantic spot. The box borders form a heart in whose upper corner a bower nestles complete with obelisk, while two giant potted plantain lilies flank the entrance. Even the flowers continue the romantic theme: the botanical name for the wonderful blue African lily (Agapanthus praecox) at the heart's centre means 'flower of love', from the Greek agape for love and anthos for flower.

Lines, strips and surfaces can all be used to divide up the surface of the garden horizontally. Vertical features are added to create a three-dimensional feel and to add interest and draw the eye around the garden. The arrangement of low-lying and vertical elements must be carefully considered by the designer in order to achieve the desired end result. What may at first sight seem merely to be a minor question of form and shape often turns out to be a significant design principle on closer examination.

Elements of design

Paths, low hedges, walls, borders and water courses cross the garden creating contours, corridors, bands and tracks, while the solid form of seats, flower beds, ponds and lawns divides and defines the garden space into sections. All these elements, the way they are used and the part they play in relation to each other and the design as a whole, contribute to the style of the finished garden.

There are two basic approaches to garden design:
• Formal style. Straight paths with precise edges and varied surfaces predominate in formal gardens, their lines and symmetry forming geometric patterns. The rectangular, square or circular sections thus formed have a steadying influence and an imposing presence.
• Freer, more natural style. Gardens like these attempt to recreate nature. Paths are laid in a gently winding manner, creating areas with natural, curving contours.

Modern gardens usually contain a mixture of styles, which generally works out well, but it is always worth experimenting to see which style suits your garden best.

Right:

A spring ribbon. Even small, delicate plants are capable of giving structure to large areas. In this naturally laid-out garden section, snowdrops (Galanthus nivalis) mark a gracefully curving, irregular path through a sea of yellow winter aconites (Eranthis hyemalis).

Left:

A strictly formal language. Time-honoured design and modern flair meet in this evergreen setting. The criss-crossing intersections so beloved of formal gardens are replaced by a modern variation: two equal beds carpeted with ivy, in which topiary box cubes add a necessary touch of height. This homogeneous design uses nothing but straight lines, rectangles and cubes, with not a curve to be seen.

Using surface and form to divide the garden

A garden's intended horizontal structure, which may appear obvious from even cursory examination of the original design plans, may not be instantly recognized by other observers, distracted by all its colourful variety. The basic feel of the garden is created by means of strip-like elements such as paths, water courses, low walls and hedges. They should divide the garden in such a way that foreground and background, the right-hand and left-hand sides and planted and empty spaces are set against one another in a balanced way.

• Narrow pools and water courses. While a natural, irregular water course is a stylistic device often used in freely designed gardens, gardens with a more formal design rely more on canal-like pools. Clearly defined borders enhance their function as stylistic devices, as does the fact that the water itself is static. As formal designs blend well with the clear-cut contours of buildings, it is advisable to install these canal-like pools with their man-made character near to buildings, ideally exactly opposite the central part of the house. Water courses, typically streams, on the other hand, if they are to be effective, evoking the feel of the countryside, need to be placed away from the house, winding their way through the garden, their uneven banks and little cascades intensifying their natural feel. If they also divide the area into unequal parts, this makes the whole garden more lively and interesting.

• Paths. Whether these divide the garden into a sharply defined area of contrasts or meander through it

Italian inspiration. Lemon trees in heavy terracotta pots line the narrow edge of the ornamental pool, evoking an Italian Renaissance garden. The pool cuts a vertical swathe through the garden, reaching almost as far as the house itself, while the citrus trees create a three-dimensional feel in this rather formal setting.

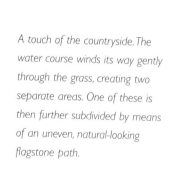

A touch of the countryside. The water course winds its way gently through the grass, creating two separate areas. One of these is then further subdivided by means of an uneven, natural-looking flagstone path.

Paths for creating order. In formal gardens, with box borders such as this one, paths can do more than just divide them up into different areas; their visual, as opposed to functional, importance puts them on an equal footing with the flower beds. A high-quality surface confirms this, such as the clinker brick in this example.

harmoniously in the form of captivating trails, they never fail to have a lasting effect on the garden's character and mood. Paths must always be considered architectural elements of central importance, not only linking different areas of the garden but also having a strong influence as artistic elements in their own right. In structured, formal gardens, the construction of straight pathways, to create a break and a contrast can be enhanced with precise edges, using topiary box hedges, lavender, cotton lavender *(Santolina)* or other border plants. The surfaces of the paths themselves can also act as counterparts to the green of the garden. While gravel, lawn and bark chippings provide multi-layered or complex plant arrangements with a steady framework, flagstones and other stone surfaces can create starkly individual visual effects, depending of course on the way they are laid. Meandering paths whose bends are planted with tall shrubs create niches and nooks which make smaller gardens look more varied and thus larger. In long, narrow gardens, paths should not run lengthwise as they will only make the garden appear even longer. However, where the path cuts through a circular flower bed, rather than installing a

Swathes of green. Grass paths are often accompanied by the classic mixed border, and not without good reason. The uniform green is a calming background, and an ideal counterbalance to the multi-coloured plantings. These distinctive grass paths run in broad swathes through the deep, perennial-filled beds.

A garden within a garden. Large gardens are usually divided into different areas which meet the different requirements of their owners. This richly planted farmer's garden comes as a pleasant surprise in the midst of these landscaped grounds which are otherwise more like a park. However, it is clear that the areas are meant to be separate; this is confirmed by the solid wooden fence, which does not have planted borders and keeps cattle at bay.

straight path, an effective alternative could be a diagonal or staggered path.

• Creating structure with different areas. The garden can be divided up horizontally using other areas like lawns, seats, ponds and flower beds, which enliven it with their contrasting surface structures and colours and yet also create their own areas of interest. Contrasting one surface with another allows you to try out the following:

▷ Green versus green. Combining the smoothly cut, mid-green grass of a lawn with bedding plants creates a pleasing effect. Grass can be coupled with the more uneven leaf textures of dark green ivy (see page 42) or pachysandra *(Pachysandra terminalis)*, with lime-green foam flower *(Tiarella cordifolia)* or browny red bugle *(Ajuga reptans* 'Atropurpurea').

Fields of tension

The garden becomes varied and interesting if busier and less-frequented spaces are not the same size, but are instead balanced as harmoniously as possible. Flower beds and seating areas belong in the former category; ornamental pools and grass in the latter.

Contrasting surfaces. This little garden has been horizontally divided into three different areas using three different surfaces. There is a strong and pleasing contrast between the petite browny-red patterning of the patio tiles, the lawn's even green and the paved seating area at the rear. However, there are also contrasts in shape as well as in materials, surface texture, patterns and colours, provided by the semi-circular grassy surface.

▷ Green versus colour. Plain surfaces such as green lawns or bedding plants can be merged with colourful flower beds to form a patchwork. Like patchwork covers, the garden will seem more unified if a single-colour framework is maintained and the same patterns are repeated rhythmically.

▷ Green or colour versus water. Ornamental pools without plants on the edges or in the water stand out against the green of the garden more effectively than natural ponds filled with a large variety of plants.

▷ Green or colour versus ground surface. Permanent seating areas or patios can be covered with small stones or laid with large slabs. They can have a uniform colour if just one material is used, or have subdued or striking patterns or combinations of colours if a mixture of materials is used. In this way, smooth and uneven surfaces combine, each enhancing the effect of the other, creating striking effects in the garden.

Surface shapes

Squares, circles, rectangles and hexagons run in no fixed direction and so have a steady, centred and focusing effect.

Uneven and long contours appear livelier, while strips and, in particular, straight lines are dynamic and purposeful.

Differences in height

Differences in height and level will liven up any surface. In small gardens, their impact is considerable. Beds, seating areas and lawns can be created on different levels, creating cosy seats and larger, raised or low-lying flower beds.

Green Walls and Backdrops

Green architecture. A green topiary corridor leads the visitor to this imposing plant temple, another area within the garden. The columned arches made from shaped beech trees change colour in autumn, showing just how versatile plants used as building materials can be.

Transforming a large and diverse range of plants into a striking gardening experience means that the design has to reach upwards. An extensive selection of vertical features is available to help you to achieve this:

• Tall plants such as trees, shrubs, climbing plants, tall herbaceous perennials and ornamental grasses.

• Garden architecture such as walls, fences, screens and trellises, pergolas, arches, obelisks, columns and pyramids. The choice and use of all of these determine the garden's proportions; whether each area or amenity is fit for purpose. The features mentioned above can be used in two ways:

▷ As a border to frame the garden, establishing a boundary and ensuring privacy and safety. While freely growing hedges will take up at least 3m (10ft) in width and are suitable only for large gardens, owners of smaller gardens can make use of narrower features such as clipped hedges, walls, fences and screens. These should not be too high, however, as the taller the enclosure, the smaller the enclosed area will appear.

▷ Vertical objects can be used to subdivide the garden, for example into the foreground, the middle and the background or into different green areas, each with their own theme or purpose. We can talk of 'staging' garden backdrops, whether using vertical backdrops, lateral inserts or divisions to create secluded areas. You can choose between more substantial borders which ensure greater privacy (such as evergreen clipped hedges or walls) or less dense screens, perhaps using deciduous shrubs or trees. Even small gardens should be subdivided. Sectioning parts of small gardens can mean a sharper focus, a better appreciation of the plants therein. Also it creates extra interest because you are unable to take it all in at one glance – there are hidden areas waiting to be discovered and enjoyed. It makes the whole garden look bigger, too.

Right:
Romantic roses. Roses wildly entwined around a pergola stimulate the imagination, as well as dividing the garden and spurring the explorer to discover what lies behind the cascade of petals.

Borders

If small gardens are surrounded by large, solid wall-like structures, a cramped, rather box-like feel is created. Topiary hedges – a kind of green wall – fences and walls should therefore be covered with climbing plants to create the illusion of depth.

Using swathes of shrubs in the foreground will also add depth. For extremely formal gardens or areas within a large garden, solid, rigid, geometrical lines can, on the other hand, function as a striking stylistic device.

These can be softened by forming clipped hedges into artistic shapes with a curved or layered silhouette, creating spheres or pyramids or medallion shapes to peer through.

Walls can be rather drab-looking or too imposing and can be pleasingly brightened up with trellised façades, especially of ornate style or with curving contours.

Top, left:
Beds to divide up spaces. Green bays, skilfully hiding parts of the garden and simultaneously drawing the gaze along a corridor, can be created by planting diagonal beds with shrubs or striking flowers, as demonstrated by this staggered herbaceous border of plantain lilies (Hosta) and phlox (Phlox paniculata hybrids).

Bottom, left:
Band of roses. Plain border hedges are transformed when medium-height shrub or bed roses are planted in front to create a truly vivid display.

Creating interest and variety

Vertical features, be they organic or non-organic, can be used to section off green havens, create backgrounds, borders or overhead displays. Lattice-work walls give the garden form and colour, and evergreen shrubs with clear-cut contours, such as topiary box spheres, pillars or cones, or scattered ornamental shrubs are equally effective dividers. Even oblong beds planted with ornamental shrubs, long-stemmed roses and attractive bedding plants or with herbaceous perennials at different heights can achieve a similar effect.

Trellises. Long narrow gardens are best divided into separate areas with diagonal trellises. Here with the floriferous rambling rose, 'Bobby James', spilling over the trellis, it forms the backdrop for this splendid flower bed of blue delphiniums, white valerian (Valeriana), pale pink bedding roses and lady's mantle (Alchemilla).

Adding height to the garden

Flowering prelude. Rose arches, like gateways, arouse a pleasurable feeling of expectation. They do not always have to adorn entrances, but can also be used throughout the garden to give a feeling of height, providing romantic views and a glorious abundance of flowers and in this way marking out a new garden area.

A few tall objects, carefully chosen and positioned, are enough to give the garden a striking feeling of space. Naturally drawing the eye onwards, it is amazing how well this device works to make the garden appear larger and create a more pleasing, three-dimensional effect.

Within the plant kingdom, trees and shrubs are best for bringing this vertical dimension into play. When choosing solitary plants, it is best to select those which will hold their own throughout the year, with attractive flowers, leaves and fruit to enhance the garden. By planting them at various

Top, right:

Creating a sense of space with individual trees. As vertical features, trees planted in staggered formation create a dramatic three-dimensional effect. Their very shape also influences the feel of the garden, and can lend it a romantic feel or a more formal air. Decorate bases with rhododendron or plantain lilies (Hosta), as in this example, and twist ivy around the trunks.

Bottom, right:

A flowering corridor. This dense leafy walkway lined with roses and clematis divides the garden and seems to be a separate room in its own right. The wrought-iron structure is attractive but can be further enhanced during the winter months by training an evergreen climber over it.

levels in the foreground, middle or background the garden will appear larger, gaining an added sense of depth.

This effect can also be created by structural supports such as rose arches, obelisks, pyramids and columns intertwined with climbing plants, such as clematis, silver lace vine, honeysuckle, climbing roses and ivy. These features will merge harmoniously with the rest of the garden if the base is disguised with different swirls of flowers or low-growing shrubs. Combining these elements by adding roofs creates another feature in the garden. Joining several plant-decked arches together forms a leafy walkway; climber-covered lattices become pergolas or bowers; and even an avenue of pillars and columns, joined together and festooned with attractive chains or ropes, can transform an other-wise dull corner.

Green Walls and Backdrops   79

ADDING MASTERFUL TOUCHES

Making ornaments, plants, stones and roots and

other decorative elements become eye-catching

features depends partly on their colour and shape but

predominantly on how they fit into the garden as

a whole. If skilfully chosen and added to the garden

scene so as not to be swamped by greenery, they

will become the sparkling jewels in the crown,

adding classical, modern, quirky, rustic,

fanciful or elegant undertones.

Garden Ornaments

Small decorative touches can help set the tone of the garden and achieve a special atmosphere. Classical and modern ornaments are striking and full of character. They can be used to create dramatic highlights, infusing whole areas of the garden with their unique character or vividly portraying a theme.

The choice is extremely wide-ranging: plant containers, amphoras, urns, vases, sculptures of animals or humans, spheres, pine cones, columns, obelisks, sundials, birdbaths or abstract sculpture. The key here is that style and location should match. In formal gardens, artistic objects can be placed at the end of a path or a line of sight, or where paths meet or in the centre of an enclosed area. In more freestyle gardens, they can be integrated into flower beds with plants twisting their way around them.

These decorative items, however, should be used sparingly; if there are too many of them, the scene will soon look too busy and cluttered. Here are just a few ideas for incorporating some of the many different garden ornaments now available:

• Coloured objects can liven up a plain green clipped hedge or add a dab of colour to beds that are not in flower.

• Light elements illuminate dark areas.

• The sometimes rather unharmonious, fussy effect of plants with small flowers and leaves is diminished by sculptures or large containers.

• Attractive vertical features such as sculptures, obelisks or vases placed on top of pillars or columns break up other larger vertical surfaces such as hedges and walls or the horizontal contours of flowerbeds or ponds. Like carefully positioned shrubs, they can also help to make the garden appear more spacious.

• Low-lying objects including animal sculptures, stone spheres and stylish plant pots draw the eye downwards, highlighting interesting detail and inviting the viewer to admire otherwise inconspicuous plants.

Mysterious and mythical. The bronze sculptures of the Scottish garden designer Dennis Fairweather are busts and plant pots in one, guaranteed to grab your attention. Each season offers a new hairstyle!

◁ Pages 80–81:

Waterworks. In formal gardens, a circular area where two paths cross creates an elegant centre of attention. A fountain spurting sculpted jets of water gives this low-lying vegetable garden a feeling of space while providing the surrounding plants with a pleasantly humid atmosphere.

Right:

Time and thyme again. Set in the midst of a sea of tiny flowers and leaves, the well-proportioned sundial directs your gaze down the centre of this herb-lined path. The sun-loving plants thyme and oregano are mixed in with aromatic lavender, golden marjoram, herb of grace, lemon balm and tarragon.

Antique garden ornaments

Antique containers and sculptures or replicas of artefacts from bygone ages are valuable aids to creating varying moods and ambiences in the garden.

❶ The clay vases and the rust patina of the urns work beautifully with the green ferns.

❷ Containers can enrich areas with their shape and material alone. This 'Mediterranean' corner benefits from the earthy tones of the amphora.

❸ Looking poised to take flight, the winged cherub cuts a romantic dash among the flowers.

❹ Like all plant pots, elegant containers (this one is made of lead) look especially attractive when foliage is allowed to spill over their edges.

❺ A magical effect is created by the silver and white cherubs reflected in the pond as they laze around its edge. The white flowers and the silver foliage of the lamb's tongue (Stachys lanata) echo the colours of the stone figures and pedestals.

❻ Amphoras provide a calming influence when situated neatly between rhododendrons and Japanese maple.

❼ The figure of a young maiden provides a visual focal point amid the wide variety of leaf shapes in this planting.

Modern ornaments

As well as purpose-made artefacts, the garden can also be embellished with second-hand items from car-boot sales or hand-made creations.

❶ Home-made deer, created from firewood.

❷ This reflective steel bird mirrors the colours of the petals that it sits amongst.

❸ A stone hen.

❹ Cast-glass perspex cones.

❺ Frogs made of silver-plated glass reflect the colours of the pond and sky.

❻ A gathering of white, cast-iron Easter bunnies.

❼ A collection of old zinc pitchers and condiments.

❽ Clay rings can be used to encircle individual plants.

Eye-Catching Plants

◁ Pages 86-87:

A fox's paradise. Even a faded flowerbed, with a little imagination, can look alive and interesting. Cast in frost-resistant bronze, these skulking foxes can withstand even the coldest winters; they will always look picturesque, whether playing on a bed of snowflakes or a summer lawn.

Striking features in the garden thrive on contrast and should have unique qualities which make them stand out from their surroundings. Because their appearance is unusual or surprising, they stop you in your tracks. This applies not just to architectural structures or sculptures, but also to plants, which do not need to be overly dominant or tower above the rest in order to steal the limelight. Many plants can become an eye-catching feature. Careful selection is the key; choosing the right plants for the designated area and presenting them so they form a contrast.

With careful thought and planning it is even possible to draw attention to lowlier plants which normally remain inconspicuous. Try cutting a lawn in concentric circles or planting marigolds in squares. Flowers grouped together in an effective manner and planted against a single-colour background are a highlight of any garden display. Many are, however, a temporary delight, losing their appeal after the flowering period comes to an end.

Evergreen woody plants and shrubs are the ideal choice for anyone who wants to create a long-lasting and effective garden display.

Closed-cone, colonnaded or umbrella conifers are important vertical features which are striking at the end of a line of sight or as fixed reference points.

Climbing plants and topiary shrubs planted as a solitary display also attract attention if their shape or colour forms an effective contrast to their surroundings.

Certain herbaceous perennials are naturally more impressive than others: good examples are the Adam's needle *(Yucca filamentosa)*, mullein *(Verbascum olympicum)*, plume poppy *(Macleaya cordata)* and ornamental crambe *(Crambe cordifolia)*, or the giant grasses like pampas grass *(Cortaderia selloana)*, Chinese silver grass *(Miscanthus sinensis)* and purple moor grass *(Molinia caerulea ssp arundinacea)*.

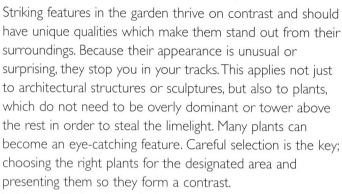

Left:

A starry moment. Topiary is the word used to describe the art of trimming evergreen plants into artificial green sculptures. Here, a cedar has been meticulously fashioned into a magnificent star whose shape will remain intact over the winter.

Right:

Spring gathering. Spring is celebrated in this garden with circles and rectangles of blue and white hyacinths. The mounted, coloured, metalic spheres echo the colours of the plants below. Their colour is so striking that the deer, keepers of the entrance to the garden, are temporarily demoted to second place. However, once the magnificent floral display has passed, they take up pole position again. The deer are fashioned from string and wire netting filled with moist peat or moss so that the climbing ivy quickly takes root, providing greenery all year round.

Unique shrubs

Like garden ornaments, individual trees and shrubs have the power to create striking visual effects. Among the so-called solitary or specimen plants (those that have the characteristics and presence to successfully stand alone), broad-leaved trees and shrubs are distinctive because of their picturesque or unusual form, their pretty flowers, decorative fruits, striking red or yellow leaves or magnificent autumn colouring. Suitable shrubs are listed below and in the boxes, according to their flowering period. Those who prefer to add a more formal touch to the garden can fall back on the enduring, contoured form of a conifer or topiary shrub. Solitary or specimen shrubs need plenty of space to create the desired effect and should not be combined with other plants.

The following broad-leaved plants are blessed with an especially beautiful form:

• Multi-stemmed plants such as the Judas tree (*Cercis siliquastrum*), katsura tree (*Cercidiphyllum japonicum*), riverbirch (*Betula nigra*) and snake-bark maple (*Acer rufinerve*).

A succinct shape. The clever terrace-like shape of this Japanese-style evergreen topiary pine makes it a focal point throughout the year. The bulbous vase situated some distance away makes for a harmonious contrast.

Right: Strong colours. An island in the pond inevitably requires a tall feature to draw attention to its unusual location. With its dense, round, crown-like shape – wider than it is high – the flaming-red Japanese maple (Acer palmatum 'Autumn fire') is perfect for the role, and particularly appreciates its damp location.

Flowering in spring

• Fragrant viburnum (+ a) (*Viburnum farreri*)
• Witch hazel (+ a) (*Hamamelis hybrids*)
• Magnolia (*Magnolia × soulangeana, M. stellata*)
• Japanese ornamental cherry (+ a) (*Prunus serrulata*)
• Flowering dogwood (+ a) (*Cornus florida*)
• Japanese crab apple (+ a) (*Malus floribunda*)
• Snowy mespilus (+ a) (*Amelanchier lamarckii*)

(+ a) with autumn colouring

Flowering in summer

• Buddleia (*Buddleia alternifolia*)
• Shrub roses (many varieties) (*Rosa*)
• Smoke tree (+ a) (*Cotinus coggygria*)
• Japanese snowball (+ a) (*Viburnum 'Plicatum' tomentosum*)
• Old man's beard (+ a) (*Chionanthus virginicus*)
• Hydrangea (*Hydrangea aspera*)

- Trailing shapes such as willow (*Salix alba* 'Tristis'), golden rain (*Laburnum* × *watereri* 'Vossii'), weeping purple beech (*Fagus sylvatica* 'Purpurea Pendula') and Camperdown elm (*Ulmus glabra* 'Camperdownii').
- Trees with a rounded crown, such as the Norway maple (*Acer platanoides* 'Globosum'), ash (*Fraxinus excelsior* 'Globosum') and mop-head robinia (*Robinia pseudoacacia* 'Umbraculifera').
- Shrubs with spreading, tiered or staggered growth such as the Japanese snowball (*Viburnum tomentosum* 'Plicatum'), dogwood (*Cornus controversa*), Japanese dogwood (*Cornus kousa*) and redvein enkianthus (*Enkianthus campanulatus*). The planting of a specimen tree or shrub can further highlight a decorative object beneath; a statue or column placed by a tall tree , a boulder or a bench at the foot of a wide-spreading shrub or a stretch of water near a weeping tree. And not forgetting the effect of a spotlight at night!

The framework does it. Even a simple plant with no imposing flowers or leaves, such as the common rush (Juncus), can become a focal point in front of the blue wall. The secret lies in the setting; the height of this unusual, dark, conical vessel echoes the shape of the grass.

Portable highlights

An impressive plant pot is the crowning accessory for any plant but should be chosen with care to ensure each complements the other. The choice of plants that suit a pot is extremely wide: richly flowering spring or summer flowers, depending on the season, or the exotic flair of Mediterranean-type plants — even roses and climbing plants can be used. Topiary box sculptures, tall-stemmed plants, small leafy shrubs and conifers should be kept in large frost-resistant containers so they can be a permanent feature of the garden, whatever the season and whatever the position of the display. When selecting a container, it is crucial that its style, shape and material blend in with the surroundings. The container can either emphasize the form of the plant or form a lively contrast to it. While flowerpots, tubs, boxes, bowls, urns,

Soft edges. With gracefully overhanging yellow-green leaves and shining blue flowers, the contrasting form and colour of the variegated blue marguerite (Felicia amelloides 'Variegata') breaks up the straight edges of the clinker terrace. The earthenware vessel blends in perfectly.

A striking pot plant. From spring to autumn, pot plants can serve as stunning garden features, but during the winter less hardy varieties will have to be kept indoors. The empty patch on the lawn can be covered with a bird house until spring comes round again. The African blue lily (Agapanthus praecox) with its 1m (3ft) high blue flowers makes the garden captivating from summer to early autumn. But at any time of year, the large clumps of evergreen strap-like leaves provide a feast for the eyes.

baskets and amphoras are mostly situated at or near ground level, directing the gaze downwards, drawing attention to horizontal focal points, plant pots placed on pillars and columns, balustrades or stairs make for outstanding high-level features, and enrich the scene with extra content, especially useful when ground space is at a premium. Pot plants provide you with a wide choice of yet more charming creative ideas for:

• Livening up shady spots, for example under shrubs or placed as an eye-catching detail in a shady seating area.

• Adding a touch of colour to beds not currently in bloom, in the middle of a lawn or a gravel area, at the centre of a crossing, at the end of a path or line of sight.

• They can look glorious when placed in enclosed floor areas: by the entrance to the house, in inner courtyards, by the edge of a pond, on pathways and in seating areas.

Olé! The scarlet Iceland poppy (Papaver nudicaule 'Matador') with its silky, crêpe cupped flowers and flaming colours really livens up this water feature throughout the summer.

Tall Highlights

Trees for arches. Two hornbeams (Carpinus betulus 'Fastigiata') planted leaving a gap in between can be grown together over a stable metal arch. In autumn, their foliage will turn to a reddish brown but will remain dense until the new spring shoots appear. The small-leaved Southern beech (Nothofagus antarctica) also makes a pretty arch and reflects the turn of the seasons with its yellow autumn colouring, while slim conifers provide a constant green.

Free-standing supports for climbing plants create a three-dimensional feel while offering so many possibilities for displaying captivating flowers or leafy green foliage to create the most striking of features. Arches, leafy walkways, pergolas, festoons, obelisks and pyramids all have their own individual creative uses and effects.

Arches

These versatile structures provide the gardener with endless possibilities. An arch can be cut like a gateway out of a topiary hedge (this should be at least 2.2m (7ft) high), from, for example, common beech (*Fagus sylvatica*), hornbeam (*Carpinus betulus* 'Fastigiata'), white cedar (*Thuja occidentalis*) or yew (*Taxus baccata*), so that it is an integral part of the hedge. Two tall shrubs can also be trained into an arch. Plant them opposite each other and then fix them together at the top. Arches like these usually tower over connecting hedges or beds, as do classic rose-covered arches on wooden or iron structures, or made from coated steel tubes or woven willow canes with horizontal, round, semicircular or pagoda-shaped curved 'roofs'.

These can be erected at the entrance to the garden, as a thoroughfare or to indicate the start of a new area of the garden. By placing four of them at the intersection of pathways, a striking centrepiece is created. When crowned with climbing plants such as roses, clematis or fragrant honeysuckle, they are transformed into a romantic feature part-obscuring but also inviting us into other areas of the garden. Arches are truly heaven-sent for small gardens, providing extra room for cascades of sweet-smelling flowers in areas where space is at a premium.

Right:

Leafy walkway. Anyone can build their own leafy walkway with the aid of several rose arches made from modern steel mesh or timber. A width of 1.8–2.5m (6–8ft) and a height of 2–3m (6½–10ft) are advisable, bearing in mind that about 30cm (12in) on either side of the path will be inaccessible due to inwardly growing plants. Complete steel mesh foliage walkway sets are available in various sizes and styles and are easily assembled.

Leafy walkways

It is the extensive number of struts linking the structure at the sides and overhead, that distinguishes the leafy walkway from a pergola. Climbing plants and shrubs can freely clamber on the structure and a floral passageway is created.

In walkways, you have a real sense of direction; even short walkways steer the visitor towards a fixed point.

At the end of the walk, a charming feature should therefore greet the eye, for example a fountain, bench, statue or bowl displayed on a pillar.

Long walkways can also be made more interesting by introducing small features at the side.

However, the frameworks can only provide generous shade quickly if vigorous climbing plants such as rambling roses, clematis or wisteria are used to cover and adorn them.

Flowery festival. The flowers of the climbing rose 'New Dawn' create a truly dazzling picture, clambering over this timber walkway, then dropping their petals to form a carpet of pink blossom. The shade-loving hortensia (Hydrangea macrophylla), planted beneath, later takes centre stage.

Wood protection and colour

Weather-resistant timber structures can be left untreated and develop a silver-grey coating over time. They can also be impregnated just like treated wood, and the treatment repeated regularly to ensure the quality of the finish — usually every two years.

Pergolas

These are generally smaller than walkways and consist of supports bearing a light roof made from crossbeams. The corner supports of less substantial structures in smaller gardens will probably be made of the same material as the roof; they need not be as sturdy as those of larger construction, which can look quite awesome, fashioned from highly decorative cast-iron, concrete, fibreglass, stone or steel and made into angular pillars or round columns. A pergola can divide the garden up into areas, for example as a gateway or wall. It can also be joined to the house or free-standing to provide shade for a seating area. While circular timber has a rustic feel, squared timber looks more functional.

Shadow games. In modern formal gardens and Asian gardens, pergolas are often not entwined with plants; and if so, only very sparingly so as not to diminish their architectural impact. The regular pattern of this imposing pergola is reflected on the ground. It forms a central feature of this garden, which makes use of rectangles of differing sizes and materials.

The climbing rose 'Dortmund' 'swings' up towards the sky from flexible supports fixed between the trees.

The poetry of the rose. Situated on arches and free-standing trellises made from blue planed timber, the vigorous, long-flowering climbing rose 'Phyllis Bide' makes a case for its yellow-pink flowers being best displayed alone.

Festoons

A garden festoon is created by positioning ornamental posts, or heavier columns or pillars, depending on the garden's size, at regular distances and hanging thick ropes or chains in between, entwined with, for example, climbing roses or clematis. This enchanting feature can be created at any height to flank paths on one or both sides. Festoons can also be used to divide the garden into other sections of any shape, charmingly framing the chosen spot.

Obelisks and pyramids

These tall features can often work wonders for even the smallest of gardens. An amazingly abundant floral display can

Climbing roses: frequently flowering

- 'New Dawn', ivory, up to 4m (13ft)
- 'Handel', cream, pink-edged, up to 3m (10ft)
- 'Gloire de Dijon', creamy buff, up to 4m (13ft)
- 'Aloha', pink, up to 3m (10ft)
- 'Sympathie', red, up to 4m (13ft)
- 'Golden Showers', yellow, up to 3m (10ft)

Striking treetops. Even old trees can be spectacularly enlivened when covered with the blooms of lax-stemmed rambling roses. These usually flower only once but lavishly, even in shady spots. It is advisable to plant them in a large tub with an open bottom, enabling them to withstand the competition of the tree roots.

Rambling roses: single flush

• 'Bobbie James' creamy white, up to 7m (23ft)
• 'Albertine', salmon-pink, with white buds, up to 5m (16ft)
• 'Apple Blossom' pale pink, up to 5m (16ft)
• 'Lykkefund' white, up to 6m (20ft)
• 'Félicité et Perpétue' cream and pink, up to 4m (13ft)

be produced in a surprisingly small area when they are used to host plants. They can be used as vertical decorative features in flower beds and can be constructed from wooden poles or coated steel tubes. For natural or country gardens, wigwams or cones woven from willow canes perform this task perfectly. In more modern gardens, it is possible to use steel or wire-netting structures.

Planting tips

Structures for supporting climbers provide for continuous floral displays if the plant varieties are chosen carefully and in light of their respective flowering times. Herbaceous perennials planted beneath, with differing flowering times, can also prolong the delightful display of colour.

The Sensual World of Water

Below, top:

Life in a wildlife pond. In late spring/early summer, dragonfly larvae climb along the plants out of the water and hatch out of their cases.

Below, bottom:

Water frogs enjoy sunning themselves on the surface of the water or on water-lily leaves that serve as lookout posts from which to catch insects.

Garden-lovers the world over have long recognized that water in all its various guises is an eye-catching feature and can perform many functions. Garden designs using water involve:
• Structure. While ponds, pools, streams and canals divide up the garden horizontally, waterfalls, water jets and fountains add height.
• Shape. Ponds and pool surfaces contrast with the straight lines of streams and canals.
• Static or dynamic. Still water in ponds, pools, swimming pools and canals reflects the sky and the surrounding area adding to the visual richness of the scene and creating a tranquil air. On the other hand, running water in streams, waterfalls and fountains is dynamic and enlivens an area of the garden.
• Sound. Flowing water creates a variety of sounds. Water trickling against stone can be heard as clearly as a murmuring stream. The quiet burbling of a water jet becomes a rushing torrent in a waterfall and a loud splashing when a tall fountain falls down into a pool.
Ornamental ponds and pools are especially striking as formal features. Suitable for modern, classical, formal or informal gardens alike, situated near to the house, or by or on a terrace, they can be displayed either at ground level or higher up, or even in a watery landscape arranged on different levels. Borders strengthen the impact of the surface but should be sparsely planted in order to preserve most of the water's reflective surface.
Natural ponds are hosts to a rich diversity of animals and plants and should therefore be laid in a quiet corner of the garden. A large surface measuring around 20sq m (215sq ft) with a richly planted area of standing water and a marshy area is required to create a balanced ecosystem. As they often merge into the green of the garden, it is wise to place striking shrubs, statues, pavilions or a waterfall on the banks to draw attention to the area.

Right:

Idyllic streams. In this open stream, the water has to steer a course through rocks and small falls, changing the speed of its flow, babbling, gurgling, murmuring in turn. The livelier effect and sounds of a mountain brook can be achieved by introducing steeper inclines, perhaps incorporating a waterfall.

▷ Pages 106–107:

Attracting wildlife. The stream is a unique and valuable feature, a graceful horizontal groove complete with its own vegetation, and gives structure to the garden. With its irregular course, becoming wider and then narrower again, it is a typical feature of informal and natural gardens. Decorating the banks with stones, and herbaceous perennials such as lady's mantle (Alchemilla mollis) and monkey musk (Mimulus luteus) will attract birds and butterflies, dragonflies and reptiles, and be a continuous scene of interest.

Water highlights

❶ Watery steps. Ideal for sloping areas where the sparkling water can tumble downwards over large natural stone barriers and into deep pools. A pretty framework of plants is important, as in this example with its ornamental grasses, bamboos and white rhododendrons.

❷ Majestic water lilies. A lush reflective frame of moisture-loving plants contributes to a splendid watery scene, of which the lilies are the undoubted focal point.

❸ A magical scene. A charming cherub statue surveying the ivy-encircled ornamental lily pond in a secluded garden retreat.

❹ Wooden bridge. This quaint rustic bridge is already covered in moss, making it more attractive to look at and imparting a romantic feel.

❺ Wooden footbridge. The solid yet softly curved footbridge echoes the rounded contours of the pond and divides up the expanse of water.

❻ Waterfall. A waterfall is always welcomed in the garden, a ceaseless visual and audial delight.

Crossings

Bridges, gangways and stepping stones are important artistic design features predominantly for use with wildlife ponds and streams in natural informal gardens as well as in Japanese-style gardens. They divide and break up the water, allow you to enjoy observing fish, vegetation and water up close, and lend house and garden a new perspective.

Bridges should never be situated towards the middle of ponds or pools but should rather be erected at the narrowest point.

Tall or bulky structures with handrails tend to blot out too much of the water's surface, reducing its size. However, if they are placed closer to the end of the pond, a larger area of the water surface remains visible, creating the illusion of greater length, leading the viewer to suppose that the pond stretches on past the bridge.

Curved bridges look especially charming when mirrored in still water, creating oval reflections. Both red-varnished Japanese bridges or an elegant white Western style is extremely attractive.

Top, left:

An inviting scene. Wooden planks laid crosswise make the straight wooden footbridge appear shorter. Reedmace (Typha) on both sides accentuates the pathway, enticing visitors to cross it and discover further delights.

Bottom, left:

Totally natural. Natural-looking stepping stones harmoniously straddle a natural pond. Placed at a maximum distance of 60cm (24in) (step size) apart, they require a solid concrete base that must be anchored to the bottom of the pond, but which should be constructed discreetly so as not to be clearly visible as this would destroy the illusion of their natural positioning. Work like this should be designed and carried out in accordance with the appropriate safety guidelines.

Large masses. Large gardens can readily accommodate large masses and shapes such as these slabs made from roughly hewn natural stone whose non-slip surface ensures maximum safety. Wet wood can be very slippery and therefore slices of tree trunks used as 'stepping stones' are best avoided.

Bottom, right:

Japanese garden. Water, gravel and stone are basic components of a Japanese garden. This attractive design is constructed from precisely hewn natural stone, rocks and small chippings.

Stepping stones placed on gravel surfaces were a favourite feature of Japanese dry gardens. They are still popular today, now placed in still and flowing stretches of water. Not only do they help to create wonderful garden scenes in different styles, they also serve to concentrate the mind while walking! Drawing the gaze downwards they encourage anyone crossing the water course to take in and appreciate more. They also set the pace of walking; a larger gap leads to quicker strides and a narrower gap to slower steps, whereas a collection of several stones makes the visitor stop and admire the scenery. Whether stone or concrete slabs, narrow oblongs or natural stone blocks, in longer paths they should be as irregular as possible, overlapping with each other or arranged in a staggered layout. They serve a decorative as well as a practical function, when placed in water in both traditional and modern gardens, and please on two levels with their mixture of materials and shapes.

Still waters

In modern gardens, the addition of water is one of the most important design components and is often used in the popular formal minimalist gardens without any distracting details or decorative ornaments. Still water in contoured pools, canals or channels, with planted borders or architectural surroundings, produces a range of effects with differently shaped surfaces and their various textures and colours. The motionless calm depths, reflective surfaces and bright ribbons of still water exude an aura of tranquillity in the garden, combining a peaceful air with a sensitive feeling for shapes, and making such a spot the ideal place for meditation.

Flat or straight elements can be used alone or combined, for example with a canal connecting two ornamental circular or rectangular ponds.

Flat elements can also be repeated several times, in

Top, left:
Surface design. This large, reflective, tranquil rectangle of water is interrupted crosswise by the smaller rectangles of the slate stepping stones. As a single tall feature, the common rush (Juncus glaucus), with its straight lines, continues the linear theme.

Bottom, left:
Effects with shapes. This design places the contrasting surfaces of water, bridge, bank and globe on different levels in relation to each other to simulate a three-dimensional abstract picture. Each feature is characterized by its own material, colour and surface: the bridge by reddish slate slabs, the edge of the bank by blue glass mosaic granules, and the swimming globe by silvery metal.

Floating gardens. Islands of plants in ornamental pools enable areas of water to be structured horizontally and vertically and offer considerable scope for the garden designer.

small gardens in the form of parallel canals, for example, or in larger grounds as opposing rectangular surfaces or as scattered round pools in the middle of a lawn, mirroring the colour of the sky like eyes.

The possibilities increase when still and flowing water are combined. Even in the tiniest of gardens, there is always space for a slit, a gully or a gargoyle in a wall or column to allow water to fall down into a small pool, as a trickle, a rivulet, jet, torrent or clear glassy curtain. Nevertheless, the resulting sounds of the water should be carefully considered.

Small amounts of water, gently dropping, create calming sounds while larger volumes of water can be stirring or even disturbing.

Attractive plants for geometrically shaped pools include round-leaved water lilies (*Nymphaea*) and water soldiers (*Stratiotes aloides*) with their sword-shaped foliage.

Water mirror. This dramatic water feature contains elements of formal baroque gardens such as water parterres, shaped shrubs and sculptures. The motionless surface of the water acts as a mirror for the statue and plants.

The Sensual World of Water

Below, left:

Close encounter. On the lawn, in the centre of a concave high-quality steel plate with a diameter of 1.5m (5ft), a crystal-like sphere made from frost-resistant, polycarbonate glass eerily revolves within a water-filled basin.

Below, middle:

Highly original. Four round, high-quality steel pools with fountains are encased in topiary box squares. Their procession-like formation catches the attention, but the sound and movement of the water is the star turn.

Modern effects with water

Water features as sculptures prove valuable additions to small and large gardens alike, showcasing water's many facets, in particular its dynamic character. Many water ornaments require so little space they can even brighten up a terrace or narrow pathway. Traditional forms such as jets, fountains, torrents or cascades also suit modern gardens as their shapes are so clear-cut.

Modern garden designers, however, do not have to leave it at that. Water can be used to stage a 'melodious concert'; dripping over different materials or flowing over a gently sloping surface from narrow gaps in parallel, spaghetti-like strands into a narrow pool. Water moving over a block or column mounted on a gravel bed or coloured glass granules will glide so softly that everything appears to shine. Or it can be used to create a screen of water to separate areas of the garden when it flows from holes from bars along curtains made of fine artificial fibres. Fashionable partners for water are currently steel, aluminium and glass, which match the water's silvery, transparent sheen, a key visual component. A steel pool filled to the brim with clear water has a strangely arresting effect and is certainly recommended for a modern garden context.

Right:

Making waves. This water sculpture is entitled 'The Wave'. The high-quality steel wall (1.5m 5ft) high and 2m (6½ft) long) really does make a wave-like ripple. Standing in a metal pool, it needs hardly any space at all and is a stunning spectacle. Seven pumps make the water run down like a watery film over the rounded edge, while the wind and changes in light cause constantly changing visual effects.

Bottom, right:

Life source. A highly unusual fountain; this bronze cactus houses a small central water jet.

Perpetual motion and sound. Thin fountains of water shoot from the mouths of four frogs placed on a corrugated base. The water splashes into the drainage channels and collects in the basin below,

while a mysterious stone relief lies at the fountain's base. The moist air produced by this romantic fountain provides the perfect growing conditions for Chinese tree peony (Paeonia suffruticosa hybrids), lady's mantle (Alchemilla mollis), golden groundsel (Ligularia dentata) and angelica (Angelica archangelica) in front of the wall covered in green-yellow ivy (Hedera helix 'Goldheart').

Traditional water ornaments

The value of water in helping to create differing atmospheres in gardens has long been recognized, and it retains its popularity to this day. Because designing with this sensory element has fascinated master gardeners and artists over the centuries, it has resulted in an extensive repertoire of imaginative settings, accessories and containers for water, including amphoras, obelisks, tanks, statues (mythical animals, fishes, dolphins, lions, cherubs and fauns), from which the water can emerge as a jet or fountain at one or more levels. In addition to this, there are some wonderful gargoyle reliefs, mostly adopted from mythology or fairy tales. These are perfect for owners of smaller gardens, as they can be fixed, along with the water supply, directly to the wall of the house, or a side wall, and only take up the space needed for a small collecting pool on the ground or on the wall. Stone fountains or Japanese water designs are also especially attractive and require little space.

Many designs from mythology, nature and fantasy are available nowadays as beautiful replicas in cast bronze, lead

Right:
A bird's paradise. A welcome drink awaits in the midst of fragrant delphinium (Delphinium), rue (Ruta graveolens), yellow-green ornamental tobacco plant (Nicotiana x sanderae), herb clary (Salvia sclarea), ornamental garlic (Allium aflatunense), white rose campion (Lychnis coronaria 'Alba') and yellow rose.

Fountain statues. A putto or cherub, coaxing a fountain of water from a fish, is often the central theme of a pond or fountain. Not only do they provide a tall feature to catch the eye, they also sometimes have a punchline which can be humorous, like this frog spurting water right in the face of the young cherub.

Below, left:

Japanese inspiration. This round fountain stone looks stunning set against cut bamboo. These stones are often placed on a gravel bed with an underground collection pool underneath.

or frost-resistant stone, fitted out with all the necessary equipment for pumping and circulating the water. Small ornamental pools in a variety of shapes are captivating, and birdbaths, attractive wells and antique-looking, wall-mounted wells can also bring magic into any garden with their still water, especially when creatively framed by plants.

Below, right:

Nostalgic. This iron pump introduces a touch of the past with its water pouring down into an old wooden churn. Pots of plantain lilies (Hosta) and coral flowers (Heuchera) provide the scene with a pretty framework.

PRACTICAL PRESENTATION

A gardener needs the right tools and materials: but from flooring surfaces, flower bed edgings, screening and walls, to compost heaps, tool sheds and vegetable plots in the kitchen garden, everything practical should look good too. Housing and displaying these items to their advantage involves some creative thinking.

Choosing Paths, Seating and Steps

◁ Pages 116–117:

Grand design. This lovely garden scene, with its grand and imposing pergola, is not on a grand country estate but is actually part of a city garden. The elaborate and ornate structure is barely concealed by the ivy, and the mirrors built into the iron framework reflect their surroundings, giving the impression of space and creating the illusion of another area of the garden existing alongside. Evergreen shrubs such as rhododendron and yew increase the garden's privacy, lending the seating area a cosy, intimate feel.

Historically, paths, seats and stairs have been viewed largely in a functional and practical light but are now rightly coming to the fore as design features as the scope of their artistic and ornamental potential is realized.

Paths and steps shape the garden with their outlines, which can be straight, arched or wavy; seating areas, with their round, angular or uneven forms also shape it. And all this is further expressed in conjunction with the individual flooring surfaces and borders.

Before researching the endless possibilities on offer, we need to consider the overall effect created as well as the practicalities. Soft surfaces such as gravel, sand, mulch or wood chips are cheap, but do not last very long, and must be regularly renewed.

In the garden, they can be used to create calming surfaces or strips of just one colour. Firmer or more stable surfaces using slabs or pavers are expensive but long-lasting and are the most varied and attractive way of enhancing the garden. Before beginning to plan, the following points should be considered:

• Foundation. Slabs and paved areas require a stable, load-bearing foundation, the depth of which will depend on the type of material used and the weight it must bear.

• Frost resistance. Stones and slabs should be weather-resistant and should exhibit no signs of cracking or flaking after frost. Suitable types include concrete, frost-resistant clinker bricks and natural stone such as granite, gneiss, basalt, porphyry, diorite and Carrara marble.

• Standing and walking safely. Smooth, polished surfaces can be slippery when wet; rough surfaces provide a better grip. Avoid using larger, obtrusive cobblestones or other surfaces with irregular and widely spaced pebble finishes for frequently used surfaces.

Below, left:
A natural mosaic. This floor, made from natural stone polygons, shows that gaps and spaces can be an important design feature.

Islands en route

Paths incorporating other smaller areas, such as squares, rectangles, circles or ovals, filled with grass, low bedding plants or herbs, which form green or scented islands, never fail to capture interest.

Right:
Elegant and enduring structures. Paths and borders mould the framework of this garden, whose character and appeal owe much to the contrast between the small pieces of irregularly laid grey granite and the uniform green border box. It is the difference in height between the flooring and the border that ensures such structures maintain their artistic impact.

Adapted to the architecture. The concrete slab floor of the path directly alongside the house is skilfully combined with cast concrete pots containing bayleaf bushes, in harmony with the style and materials of the house. As with traditional leafy walkways, a visual treat awaits the visitor at the end of this modern columned walkway: the flooring also perfectly complements the wall fountain and pool.

Flooring surfaces for paths and seating areas

While in natural gardens, or at the edges of larger gardens, paths and seating areas can be covered with permeable, inexpensive materials such as gravel, sand, mulch and wood chips, it is more practical to lay frequently used and visually prominent paths and seating areas with more functional yet decorative materials. This applies, for example, to house entrances, which are the first things that are seen and thus make the all-important first impression on visitors. It is also important with patios and all small gardens feature, where design flaws are immediately visible. It is therefore advisable not to cut costs too heavily by saving on materials or professional assistance, as this would put at risk safe, lasting quality. The decorative result can then be admired day after day, whatever the season, for decades to come. Your imagination can be left to run wild, thanks to the huge range of possibilities created by the wide choice of materials and shapes, such as clinker and wood, natural stone and

Lively surfaces. You do not need many plants to bring variety to an inner courtyard. Here, the floor surface is a highly decorative feature: exposed aggregate concrete bordered with rows of pebbles and clinkers laid flat and on end. The carpet of lesser periwinkles (Vinca minor) under the maple looks stunning in spring with its sky-blue flowers.

A calming path. The narrow concrete path, made with different sizes of cobbles, weaves its way between the colourful and diverse flowers which spill on to it and soften its lines.

concrete, which are available as rectangular, square or polygonal slabs as well as cobblestones in varying sizes. These materials can be used to structure the surfaces in numerous ways (formations), be combined to create patterns or introduce variety to surfaces with scattered mosaics of contrasting materials. The following points should be taken into account:

• The material, format and pattern should not conflict with the house, garden and plants.

• Smaller areas and narrow paths work best with smaller, individual paving stones and narrow gaps.

• Large areas and wide paths look spacious with slabs and consistent use of materials.

• Long paths appear wider and shorter when the materials are laid diagonally; short paths are best laid lengthways.

• Brighter floor coverings can be blinding in sunny areas but can help to lighten shady areas.

An eye-catching patchwork. The smaller the area, the livelier and more detailed the surface can be. Here, an edging of different-sized concrete slabs harmoniously offsets the colourful mosaic in the middle. Its refreshing effect is created by the mixture of small clinker bricks, different natural cobblestones and coloured, frost-resistant ceramic stones. With its irregular contours, it tends to draw your attention away from the otherwise imposing tall flower-bed borders.

Nature gaining ground. Avoiding precise divisions between the flowerbeds and path creates a natural-looking effect that is just right for a romantic, wild garden. Here, the natural stone slab pathway illustrates this beautifully, allowing plants such as the silver-grey spiked speedweed (Pseudolysimachion spicatum ssp. incanum) to establish themselves in the gaps.

Edges and borders

Idyllic country garden. Gravel path with a flower-bed border of colourfully leaved, yellow-flowering nasturtiums (Tropaeolum majus 'Alaska Gold').

Flower beds can either be kept separate from paths or the two can be allowed to merge together, depending on the garden's particular style.

Edgings can be useful as well as having a visual function. High-edged stone borders can be used to contain loose surface coverings (such as gravel or sand) or a paved area (see pages. 6–7,) or allow you to create raised plant beds (see pages. 11, 121 right).

On the other hand, stones placed at ground level widen walkways, emphasizing their course (see page 119) and have the advantage of allowing lawns to be mown right up to the edge.

Pretty borders can also be created around curving paths by using frost-resistant clinker bricks or cobblestones laid end-up and embedded in concrete. Concrete slabs are also suitable for straight paths.

Flexible metal or plastic edging strips are very popular in England, slightly raised, for bordering and clearly outlining the edges of lawns. For forest pathways and country gardens, wooden planks or circular wood can be used which blend in well with the surrounding natural features.

Right:

Separator. The double row of clinker bricks prevents the gravel from the path mixing with the earth from the flower bed. But it doesn't stop the flowers such as dahlias attractively spreading on to the path.

Doubly framed. At the central crossing of this garden a granite cobble border traces the shape of the crossing. The opulent frames of the four central flower beds with white-flowering feverfew add structure to the whole, while freely flourishing lavender bushes form the outer frame.

City gardens and small gardens, however, are enhanced by stylish ornamental border stones (for example with a corded edge) that can also be purchased in concrete, stone or frost-resistant clay in traditional and modern designs. Old-fashioned metal railings or low wicker fences can be placed in the earth to define planted areas. But plants, too, can form charming flower-bed borders, either left free to merge into the pathway, as with freely designed gardens, or precisely ordered. The darling of all formal gardens and a common favourite, the trimmed box, provides vivid outlines even in the winter.

Below, middle:
Mounted in green. The green border stands out well against the earthy red tones of the clinker brick path.

Below, right:
Natural deception. This spot in the garden has been skilfully created to make it look like a natural woodland scene, with its mulched path and plants which are left to grow on to it.

Steps with flair

① Iron steps have an airy and decorative effect and can bridge problem areas.

② Small wooden steps help to overcome the slope of this rustic raised garden.

③ Curved steps are an artistic eye-catcher and are easier to lay with smaller cobblestones than with slabs.

④ Steps always blend in harmoniously with the garden when they echo the materials of their surroundings, such as these large edging rocks.

⑤ Sweeping steps bordered by trimmed box make such an elegant statement.

⑥ Old sleepers gain new glory with ivy growing between each step and merging into the border.

⑦ Broad, low steps are individually edged with a contrasting stone and the green borders overgrow the edges.

Elegant Screening

As most gardens are located in close proximity to houses and other gardens, you must confront the problem of how to maintain privacy. Fortunately, there are many solutions available, allowing you to make a virtue out of necessity and achieve the desired objective using materials which can also become eye-catching features. It is crucial to remember that high wood fences are not the only answer to this issue; there are more stylish, subtle screens available for the boundary, seating area or patio that come in varying heights, materials and design detail. Choose carefully to be sure the screening blends into the garden.

A plain, smooth concrete wall can successfully imitate the minimalist style of a modern house and give the perfect finishing touch to the plants in front of it but could appear bare and unfriendly in other settings. Small terraced house gardens visible from all sides should not be 'hermetically sealed' with a single structure, but should rather use a combination of space-saving devices that also add a bit of variety. When deciding exactly how to achieve this, you should also consider whether protection from the wind and noise are necessary as well as privacy from the side, or even from above if you are overlooked by surrounding houses.

On the patio, to prevent being observed from above you can use attractive awnings or covered pergolas. In the garden, this can also be achieved with an arbour romantically covered with climbing plants or a tall or even small tree with a broad crown.

Evergreens and large or densely growing hedges help block out wind and sound. A wall can add individual charm to the garden when decorated using colourful touches: wood, stone mosaics or trellises with climbing plants.

• Free-growing hedges can often be used to achieve privacy in large gardens. Depending on the density of screening required, they can be planted in rows one to three deep with a total width of 3–5m (10–16ft). If appropriate to the style of the garden, a natural hedge could be created to mirror a

Airy protection. Made from brick and concrete stones, this perforated wall lets the air in, you can look through it, and it can be of any colour. In hotter regions, this wall does not heat up as much as a closed one because the air can circulate, creating a pleasant microclimate. A particularly ornamental lattice look can be created by using different-shaped stones.

Right: Covered in roses. Specialist suppliers offer a wide range of beautifully shaped old-fashioned railings which provide the perfect place for climbing roses to take hold. The rails also serve as an attractive feature in the winter when the leaves and flowers no longer screen the garden.

Illusions. The slightly angled mirror breaks up the uniformity of the small-leaved green hedge, creating the illusion of a broad-leaved tree which is then reflected in the mirror-like water.

country hedgerow containing a variety of wild plants; or choose elegant mixed flowering hedges that follow the seasons with their changing flowers. Shrubs planted between hedges can also ensure a certain amount of privacy even in winter, while evergreen hedges of, say, rhododendrons guarantee year-round protection.

• In small gardens, the practical will likely go hand in hand with

Stretching the imagination. Blue surfaces made from nylon fabric and stretched between posts boldly screen off two very different areas of the garden.

Privacy and pleasure

Barriers created by forming small apple or pear trees into hedges, or training apricots, peaches or plums to entwine on a free-standing trellis, mean that these screens can also be part of the autumn harvest. Blackberries and peas also look wonderful trained over elegant railings, while runner beans quickly entwine themselves around the upright supports.

Green-shaped screen. This green open-work screen has a highly original look, with ivy on large frames providing year-long greenery, and the flowering clematis adding its own magic. The umbrella-shaped clipped yews, like the ivy, bring both structure and style to the garden even in winter.

the decorative, and yet need not take up too much space. Topiary screening fashioned from conifers such as yew (*Taxus*), cypress (*Chamaecyparis*) and cedar (*Cedrus*) provide a relaxing framework, remaining green all year round. Hornbeams (*Carpinus betulus*) and beech (*Fagus sylvatica*) follow the seasons with their changing leaf colours in autumn and fresh green foliage in spring. Yews take up the least space; they can be just 50cm (20in) wide and can also be cut to create openings you can see through, or shaped to make sculptures.

While willow or reed fence panels last for about 10 years, the treated wooden screening of pergolas are more durable. Climbing roses, clematis and honeysuckle can be trained over them to provide a romantic medley of flowers. Shady areas are particularly suitable for evergreen ivy. Terraced house gardens often have patio walls to ensure privacy and these can be used in a variety of ways: try decorating them with trellises for climbing plants, using them as a supporting surface for potted gardens, perking them up by encorporating an attractive mosaic or relief here or there, or even installing a small water feature that will add bubbling energy to the patio as well as raise the humidity level.

Privacy and illusion

In small gardens, optical illusions can be created to give a sense of extra space. Mirrors built into pergolas, rose arches or trellises fixed to a wall deceive you into thinking you can glimpse and enter another part of the garden.

Paintings and murals on walls and screens can also create the illusion of depth leading the eye onward into another dimension.

Privacy and details

Long shaped, screening hedges should be broken up with an ornament such as a statue or vase on a pillar. This will stop them becoming oppressive. Alternatively the uniform lines of the hedging could be interrupted by a decorative garden highlight, for example an arbour with bench, a rose arch with a closed backdrop or a decorated pavilion.

Artful Disguise

A successful garden is not only an attractive place for leisure and pleasure; it is also the gardener's workplace housing tools and fertilizers.

It is a nurturing place for young plants, a watering hole for garden wildlife and a collection area for garden waste and compost.

It is also sometimes home to numerous other kinds of objects belonging to the owner such as dustbins, bicycles or even the car. In other words, it has to incorporate many practical things that may have nothing to do with the garden. Avoid eyesores by maintaining garden storerooms and disguising them artfully.

Summer houses and sheds

The importance that these storerooms for lawn-mowers, garden tools, pots and fertilizers, garden furniture and so on often have for the gardener is not always reflected in their appearance. Often neglected, they can spoil a corner of the garden or are instead attached any old how to the house or garage.

The question is, why not invest the same time and effort here as with your plants? – you will soon see the benefits. With a little imagination, there are many ways in which summer houses and sheds can be transformed into stylish garden features in no time at all:

• Painting or varnishing, in any of a range of decorative colours, will either match the house or make the shed stand out as an attractive feature.

• By using mouldings and trimmings on doors and windows, plain sheds can be transformed into a pièce de résistance with a decorated gable front in a contrasting colour or with a roof covered with real roof tiles in place of roofing felt. Doors and windows can make use of pretty lattice shapes and attractive handles; wooden doors can be ornamented.

• Using greenery: plants should help integrate the shed or

Practical yet good-looking. Imagination is essential even in the practical maintenance department of the garden. The outer wall of a shed or summer house can be beautifully decorated with old tools.

Right:

The art of trelliswork. Elaborate trellis façades provide the perfect framework for climbing plants. In this example, even the load-bearing columns can accommodate plants, while the wall trellises perform a clever optical illusion making the arches seem to curve inwards. Although potential climbing aids, these are primarily ornamental façades and should not therefore be completely covered in greenery.

summer house into the garden. Make sure the shed has a new coat of paint then place flower boxes at the windows and hanging flowerpots on awnings and flank the entrance with potted plants or climbing plants on trellises.

• Suitably placed external illumination will light up the shed, improving its looks and making for increased security.

Unsightly façades and walls

The drab walls of functional outbuildings such as garages often face directly on to the garden. Unadorned walls above narrow pathways or the neglected walls of old buildings can also look dismal. However, all this can be changed for the better through the use of artistic trellises. Thanks to the sheer range of garden architecture available, such as arches, portals and gables, which can also be combined with each other, surfaces of all kinds can be structured in a delightful manner or even have their proportions improved. Generally available in white, green, blue and black, they can also be painted to match the colour of the house or garden. These frames often look so striking afterwards that dense planting is no longer necessary or even desirable.

Dustbins

Disguise or concealment is the usual remedy when it comes to these eyesores. They can simply be placed out of view behind evergreen topiary cedar, yew, cherry laurel or privet hedges, or in a wooden bower painted with colours that match the house and garden and covered with climbing plants such as roses, clematis, Virginia creeper, ivy, climbing hortensia or annual hops. Those who prefer to keep their waste bags or bins in a closed brick or wooden structure can

Top, left:
Magnificent plants at the entrance to the house. Its powerful aerial roots have allowed the evergreen spindle tree (Euonymus fortunei 'Emerald 'n Gold') to hide the old walls under a coat of dense yellow-green foliage.

Middle, left:
Sweet pea wigwam. The delicately fragranced annual sweet pea (Lathyrus odoratus) has gracefully taken over the tent-like structure, hiding the compost bin and helping it integrate into the greenery of the garden.

Bottom, left:
Mobile screening. Climbing plants such as Virginia creeper (Parthenocissus quinquefolia) and ivy (Hedera helix), kept in plant tubs, can be trained into mighty columns which are almost big enough to hide parked cars.

Top, right:

Wall dressing. What better way to cover a large wall in a sunny area of the garden than with climbing roses. Alternatively, ivy (Hedera helix) and climbing hydrangea (Hydrangea anomala ssp. petiolaris) will work well in shady areas.

Middle, right:

Green roof. Whether belonging to a summer house or storage area, garage or carport, the roof is never too steep for a mini-biosphere. Before planting, however, the roof must be suitably protected.

Bottom, right:

Edible screen. Fast-growing runner beans wind themselves around thick ropes or canes and can hide any unsightly areas of the garden. Scarlet runner beans (such as the 'Lady Di' variety) delight with their striking reddish blooms and edible pods.

paint this in a fitting colour or cover it with climbing plants.

Compost

Trellises entwined with climbing plants or ramblers can conceal compost areas as effectively as topiary hedges. In rural gardens, robust shrubs such as elder or forsythia, sunflowers, hollyhocks and foxgloves are also suitable for planting near compost areas. For the country garden look, why not use pumpkins and nasturtiums?

Water

Rainwater is very good for watering your plants and also looks attractive when collected in pretty pools, wooden casks or natural stone troughs rather than stored in unattractive plastic containers.

Stylish Kitchen Gardens

Ever since the late Rosemary Verey, celebrated English gardening author and designer, revealed her artistic kitchen garden to an appreciative general public, the word within those circles has been that 'beautiful' and 'practical' are not incompatibles.

The idea of using vegetables, herbs and fruit as ornamental garden design elements is more popular than ever, especially with those who want to grow and cook their own produce but have small gardens. The intention is not necessarily an elaborate self-sufficient garden but rather an attractively arranged one which will bring variety into the kitchen, especially with new varieties of plants or forgotten or previously unknown species.

This is also possible in small gardens and even in a potted garden, as a little of everything is sufficient. The important factor here is that the plants are attractive to look at as soon as they are put into their beds, even when combined with flowers and herbs.

• Taller plants prevent tedious carpet-like beds. Just allow runner beans to grow up canes and arches, and tomatoes and climbing strawberries to develop their succulent red fruits on posts, poles, obelisks or pyramids. Long-stemmed berry plants and slender apple or pear trees or column-like ballerina apple varieties will also be the highlight of any bed. Grapevines, blackberries, peas or runner beans can be trained upwards over bowers or pavilions in the middle of a sunny garden or attached to attractive open-work walls to provide effective screening.

• With a border of herbs such as chives, lavender, parsley, garlic, cotton lavender (*Santolina chamaecyparissus*), curry plant (*Helichrysum italicum*), rue (*Ruta graveolens*) or garden nasturtium (*Tropaeolum majus*) a truly magical plot can be created. Radishes, colourfully leaved salads and even red cabbage can add charm to pathways.

• As individual elements within a plot, suitably tall-growing plants include the imposing sea kale (*Crambe cordifolia*),

artichokes, globe artichoke (*Cynara scolymus*), bronze fennel (*Foeniculum vulgare* 'Atropurpureum') or angelica (*Angelica archangelica*) with its yellow-green umbel flowers on tall reddish stems.

• Low-growing vegetables and herbs can also stand out when placed in an impressive pot. Examples include frost-sensitive herbs such as rosemary and lemon grass, as well as courgettes, which will spill out over the edge of the pot, rich red-white flowering scarlet runner beans ('Hestia'), extremely decorative blue-green palm cabbages ('Nero di Toscana') or strawberries in striking strawberry planters.

• Colourfully leaved vegetables and herbs ensure that there is plenty of colour in the bed even without an abundance of flowers. It is worth reading up on the wide range of varieties available: learn of yellow-green and red-leaved lettuces, green and blue broccoli or kohlrabi, red or white spring onions, red- or green-leaved beetroot, the striking grey-green of onions and white cabbage as well as the blue-purple of the red cabbage. Sensational colour is provided every time by the metre- (3ft-) high red-leaved cabbage 'Redbor', the glowing red cultivated orache (*Atriplex hortensis*) or the red-stemmed beet ('Feurio' or 'Vulkan').

Herbs also have red-green and yellow-green varieties and, more importantly, silver-grey leaves that mediate wonderfully between stark contrasts.

Design tips

As edible plants are intended for consumption, many only have a relatively short stay in the bed. This gives the gardener the opportunity to constantly design new combinations over the course of the year. Vegetables can be cultivated in ornamental carpet-like beds or arranged at different heights just like beds of shrubs.

It is of course important to maintain easy access for cultivating and harvesting. In order to avoid making mistakes

Colourful carpet. Beginners who want to practise their garden designs could take colourful leafy vegetables as their starting point.

A change of height. Decorative apple espaliers and lavender borders frame this onion and lettuce vegetable plot. The fragrant lavender flowers add colour to the greenery.

Colourful experiment. Vegetable gardeners can also experiment with colours and leaf textures at the same time, as shown here with carrots, lettuce, red cabbage, onions, beetroot and blue kohlrabi.

Bleaching. These 'planters' do not only add visual interest. The dandelion and sea kale (Crambe maritima) shoots therein become bleached and can be cut and prepared like asparagus. In order to avoid weakening the plants, only a part of the stalk should be removed.

right from the start, it is advisable to check combinations in
specialist tables as some vegetable plants and herbs are
incompatible and can adversely affect the growth of others,
whereas others actually have a positive effect. If there is little
room for a kitchen garden, vegetable and fruit plants can be
kept in large containers on terraces or patios.

Bed roses or summer flowers are also useful when
arranging kitchen garden plots.

Framing borders of roses, borders, cones or spheres made
of box, or using ornaments or garden architecture, ensures
that the kitchen garden will be attractive all year round.

▷ Page 138:

*A colourful mixture of vegetables
and flowers. The bed is framed
by runner beans and white-
flowering peas. As well as
flowers, the wrinkly red lettuce,
red cabbage leaves and the red-
stalked leaf mangold greatly
contribute to the overall effect.*

Appendix

Garden Owners and Garden Creators

a = above, b = below, m = middle,
l = left, r = right;
D = designer, O = owner,
CFS = Chelsea Flower Show

p. 2–3 D: Jürgen Papenfuss & Jürgen Rösner; p. 11 D: Stephen Woodhams; p. 12 D: Dan Pearson (Evening Standard Garden) CFS; p. 13 D: Rosemary Verey; p. 14 a D/O "Homestead Inn", Greenwich Conn. USA; p. 16 a D/O Jürgen & Renate Scholz; p. 16 l D: Jürgen Papenfuss & Jürgen Rösner; p. 16 bl D: Barbara Hammerstein; p. 16 br D: Whitchford Pottery; p. 17 O: Gabriele & Stephan Christensen; p. 18 D/O: Sir Terence Conran; p. 20 a D: Wolfgang Oehme & James van Sweden; p. 20 l and p. 21 a D/O: Jürgen & Renate Scholz; p. 21 b D/O: Rolf Walter Schwarze; p. 22 D/O: Christiane Widmayr-Falconi & Monika Tittlbach; p. 23 a D/O: Johanna Korte-Mels; p. 23 m D: Rosemary Verey; p. 23 b: Sissinghurst; p. 24 (all) D/O: Ralf Lippke; p. 25 al D: Jürgen Papenfuss & Jürgen Rösner; p. 25 ar D/O: Sir Roy Strong & Dr. Julia Trevelyan-Oman; p. 25 b O: Hildegard Osterauer; p. 26 D/O: Gudrun & Friedrich-Karl Meyer; p. 27 D/O: Dorothee & Karl Heinz Tümmers; p. 28 D: Carole Vincent (Blue Circle Garden) CFS; p. 29 a D: Wolfgang Oehme & James van Sweden; p. 29 b D: Andy Sturgeon (Circ Garden) CFS; p. 30 D: Andrew Crace; p. 31 D/O: Barbara Hammerstein; p. 32 l D/O: Gudrun & Friedrich-Karl Meyer; p. 32 bl O: Gisela & Herman Rudolph; p. 32 bm D: Phillip Watson, Washington Gardens; p. 32 br D/O: Erika Jahnke; p. 33 D: Bunny Guinness, CFS; p. 34 D/O: Karl & Maria Artmeyer; p. 35 D/O: Jürgen & Renate Scholz; p. 36 a D/O: Gisela & Wolfgang Hecking; p. 36 b D/O: Gudrun & Friedrich-Karl Meyer; p. 37 b O: Gisela Haidacher; p. 38/39 Rosarium Sangerhausen; p. 40 D: Hiroshi Nanamori (Goa Garden) CFS; p. 42 a and p. 43 a D: Jürgen Papenfuss & Jürgen Rösner; p. 42 b D/O: Lorenz von Ehren; p. 43 b D: Joachim Winkler; p. 44 and p. 45 a O: Fee Höfermann, D: Angela Ernst; p. 45 b D: Jürgen Papenfuss & Jürgen Rösner; p. 46–47 D: Re-Nature, Ruhwinkel; p. 49 O: Fee Höfermann, D: Angela Ernst; p. 50 a Chenies Manor, Rickmansworth, D: Elizabeth MacLeod-Mathews; p. 50 b D/O: Rolf Walter Schwarze; p. 51 a D/O: Erika Jahnke; p. 51 b D/O: Uta & Stephan Kirchner, Kleiseerkoog; p. 52 a D: Jürgen Papenfuss & Jürgen Rösner; p. 52 b O: Birgit Hardinghaus; p. 53 D: Jürgen Papenfuss & Jürgen Rösner; p. 54–55 Chenies Manor, Rickmansworth D: Elizabeth Macleod-Mathews; p. 56 ar D: Jürgen Papenfuss & Jürgen Rösner; p. 56 bl D: James Alexander-Sinclair (The Express Garden) CFS; p. 57 a D/O: Ursula & Klaas Schnitzke-Spijker; p. 57 bl D: Peter Styles (Blakedown Landscapes Garden) CFS; p. 57 br D: Claire Whitehouse (St Barts Garden) CFS; p. 58 D/O: Renate Richl; p. 59 Chenies Manor, Rickmansworth D: Elizabeth Macleod-Mathews; p. 60 D: Mark Anthony Walker (Cartier Garden "A City Space") CFS; p. 61 D/O: Ulrike & Rainer Dammers; p. 62 D: Ian Taylor, spidergarden.com (a: Mother Earth Garden, b: Zen Inspired Garden) CFS; p. 63 a D: Stephen Woodhams (The Marks & Spencer Cut Grass Garden) CFS; p. 63 b D: Michael Balston (Daily Telegraph Garden) CFS; p. 64 D: Ulrich & Hannelore Timm; p. 65 D: Henk Weijers; p. 66/67 D: Diana Ross, London; p. 68 D/O: Caroline Menzel; p. 70 D/O: Rolf Walter Schwarze; p. 71 a D: Joachim Winkler; p. 71 bl D/O: Brigitte & Jürgen Hummel & Marianne & Stefan Blume; p. 71 br D/O: Gisela Haidacher; p. 72 D/O: Maria Mattheisson, Long Island; p. 73 D/O: Johanna Korte-Mels; p. 74 D/O: Rolf Walter Schwarze; p. 75 D/O: Margot

von Winkler; p. 76 a D/O: Caroline Menzel; p. 76 b D: Jürgen Papenfuss & Jürgen Rösner; p. 77 D/O: Ursula & Klaas Schnitzke-Spijker; p. 78 O: Sigrid & Heiko Ashenbeck; p. 79 a D/O: Ralf Lippke; p. 79 b D/O: Ursula & Klaas Schnitzke-Spijker; p. 80–81 D: Marc Schoellen, Luxembourg; p. 82 D: Dennis Fairweather; p. 83 D/O: Jane & Peter Dunn, Stone House, Rushlake Green; p. 84 a D/O: Rolf Walter Schwarze; p. 84 bl D/O: Margot & Bernd Werno-Strobl; p. 84 m D: Cherida Seago (Reclaimed Garden) CFS; p. 85 bl D/O: Familie Born DiTerra, Hamburg; p. 85 br D/O: Sigrid Braun; p. 86/87 D: David Seeler, The Bayberry, Sagaponack NY; p. 88 al D/O: Barbara Hammerstein; p. 88 ar and br D/O: Uta & Stephan Kirchner, Kleiseerkoog; p. 88 m D/O: Marlies Tubes; p. 88 bl D: Stephen Woodhams; p. 89 a D/O: Uta & Stephan Kirchner, Kleiseerkoog; p. 89 bl D/O: Marc de Winter; p. 89 br D: Whitchford Pottery; p. 90 D: David Seeler, The Bayberry, Sagaponack NY; p. 91 D/O: Uta & Stephan Kirchner, Kleiseerkoog; p. 92 D/O: Lorenz von Ehren; p. 93 D/O: Jane & Peter Dunn, Stone House, Rushlake Green; p. 94 a D: Cleve West & Johnny Woodford (A Garden For Learning, Merrill Lynch) CFS; p. 95 a D/O: Diana Ross, London; p. 95 b D: Arabella Lennox-Boyd (Evening Standard Garden) CFS; p. 96 D: Joachim Winkler; p. 98 D/O: David Seeler & Ngaere McCray, Sagaponack NY; p. 99 D: Chris Moore, Jack Chandler & Associates CA; p. 100 l: Rosarium Sangerhausen; p. 100–101 m D/O: Sir Roy Strong & Dr. Julia Trevelyan-Oman; p. 101 r D/O: Ursula & Klaas Schnitzke-Spijker; p. 103 D/O: Elke & Reinhold Lunow; p. 104 al D: Wolfgang Eberts; p. 105 bl D/O: Hannelore & Jürgen Gerber; p. 105 br D: Henk Weijers; p. 106–107 D/O: Elke & Reinhold Lunow; p. 108 a D: Gudrun & Friedrich-Karl Meyer; p. 109 a D/O: Elke & Reinhold Lunow; p. 109 b D: Hiroshi Nanamori (Goa Garden) CFS; p. 110 a D: David Stevens (Daily Telegraph Garden) CFS; p. 110 b D: Alan Sargent (Silver Reflections Garden) CFS; p. 111 a D: Arabella Lennox-Boyd (A Garden for all Time) CFS; p. 111 b D: George Carter (Christies Garden) CFS; p. 112 l D: Allison Armour (The Garden of Reflection) CFS; p. 112 m D: Arne Maynard & Piet Oudolf (Evolution, Gardens Illustrated; fountain by James Elliott) CFS; p. 112 r D: Alan Wilson, The Sculpture Workshop; p. 113 D: Alan Wilson, The Sculpture Workshop; p. 114 a D/O: Maria Mattheisson, Long Island; p. 115 a D: Rosemary Verey; p. 115 bl D: Wolfgang Eberts; p. 115 br D: Jane Adams (Home Farm Trust Garden) CFS; p. 116–117 D: Ulrich & Hannelore Timm; p. 119 D/O: Ralf Lippke; p. 120 l D/O: Marietrud & Reinhard Buck; p. 120 r D: Wolfgang Niemeyer; p. 121 r O: Renate & Dieter Hansen, D: Avant Gardeners; p. 122 a D/O: Ursula & Klaas Schnitzke-Spijker; p. 122 b D: Jeff Goundrill (The Garden of Eden) CFS; p. 123 a D/O: Jürgen & Renate Scholz; p. 123 bl D: Jürgen Papenfuss & Jürgen Rösner; p. 123 bm D/O: Uta & Stephan Kirchner, Kleiseerkoog; p. 123 br D: Joachim Winkler; p. 124 al D/O: Packwood House Garden; p. 124 m D/O: Gisela & Wolfgang Hecking; p. 124 bl D/O: Jürgen & Renate Scholz; p. 125 al D: Mark Anthony Walker (Tribute to Vita Sackville West Garden) CFS; p. 125 ar D/O: Gerda & Jürgen Zwickel; p. 125 b D/O: Ursula & Klaas Schnitzke-Spijker; p. 127 Rosarium Sangerhausen; p. 128 a D: Tom Stuart-Smith (A Garden in Homage to Le Nôtre) CFS; p. 128 b D: Andy Sturgeon (Circ Garden) CFS; p. 129 Chenies Manor, Rickmansworth D: Elizabeth MacLeod-Mathews; p. 130 D/O: Ursula & Klaas Schnitzke-Spijker; p. 132 m D: Michael Miller (Cartier/Harpers & Queen Garden, Impressions of Highgrove) CFS; p. 113 m D: Re-Nature, Ruhwinkel; p. 136 am D/O: Jane & Peter Dunn, Stone House, Rushlake Green; p. 136 bm D: Jeff Goundrill (The Garden of Eden) CFS; p. 137 D: Rosemary Verey; p. 138 D: Rupert Golby (Country Living Magazine Garden) CFS

Glossary

accent plant - Any plant that is used to draw the eye in a bed or border or in a container. Accents might be created with tall plants in a mostly low-growing border or a spreading plant on an otherwise unadorned lawn.

annual - A plant that grows, flowers, produces seed and dies in one growing season - spring to autumn or winter. Some plants that cannot survive frosty weather without protection, such as canna lilies, are often grown as annuals and then discarded, even though they could survive for many more years.

architectural plant - A plant with a striking shape, such as a weeping tree, or an interesting leaf form, such as spiky or huge and glossy. Architectural plants are often used for accents.

bedding plant - Usually annuals, grown for their flowers or attractive foliage, bedding plants are used en masse to create a vivid but short-lived display. Although they are associated with large flowerbeds, such as those in municipal parks, they can be used successfully in private gardens, too. Common bedding plants are primulas and wallflowers in spring plantings and salvias and canna lilies in summer displays.

biennial - A plant that survives two years, growing in the first year and producing flowers and seeds in the following year before dying. Some plants, such as wallflowers, are grown as biennials, even though they are capable of living for longer.

bulb - A bulb is a storage organ, usually underground, from which a plant can grow. Bulbs are made up of numerous leaves or leaf-like structures wrapped around each other and getting smaller towards the bulb centre. Onions and daffodils are bulbs.

compost - vegetative material from the kitchen and garden that is rotted down and then used to improve the quality of all soils. A good compost heap is made of a mixture of coarse material, such as vegetable peelings and green stems, and finer material, such as grass clippings and seedling weeds. Good compost is virtually odourless or smells quite pleasant. Always mix grass clippings in well with other material to prevent them clumping together in a smelly mass.

corm - Like a bulb, a corm is a storage organ like a squashed fleshy stem from which a plant can grow. Cyclamen, crocuses and montbretia are corms.

crown - Herbaceous perennials die down to a crown and roots in the winter. The crown is the cluster of dormant buds at the soil surface that will produce the next year's plant.

cultivar - A cultivar is a plant that varies in some way from the species to which it is related, perhaps having bigger flowers or being smaller or larger in growth. 'Cultivar' is short for 'cultivated variety'; cultivars are usually plants that have been deliberately bred or selected in gardens or nurseries. For example, the cultivar *Salvia patens* 'Cambridge Blue' has pale blue flowers, whereas those of the species, *Salvia patens*, are rich dark blue.

evergreen - An evergreen plant is one that is never without leaves at any point in the year. Perennials, shrubs and trees can all be evergreen.

fleece - Thin horticultural sheeting used to protect seedlings and frost-vulnerable plants.

formal garden - Any garden that has a strong structure and repeated shapes. Formal gardens are usually kept extremely neat and tidy. Formality can be created with patterned layouts, such as knot gardens and parterres, clipped plant shapes, like box *(Buxus)* or other hedging, and strong architectural features, such as paths and walls, and so on.

framework - In a garden, the framework is the underlying structure, the evergreens, the deciduous trees and the paths and other features, that will be visible in some form all year round.

gazebo - From the Persian meaning a platform to view the moon, a gazebo is a an enclosed, roofed structure, such as a summerhouse, often circular or hexagonal, and usually intended for sitting beneath.

genus - A plant genus (for example *Geranium*) consists of a group of plants that share a number of characteristics, such as flower appearance, general leaf shape, root structure and so on. The plural form is genera.

graft - A graft is produced when a shoot or part of a shoot of one plant is joined to the roots of another. Grafts are common in fruit trees, such as apples, because they enable the breeder to ensure that a tree will grow strongly but be of a predictable size, such as dwarf or medium. Ornamentals, such as roses, may be grafted to produce a plant of a reasonable size more quickly than it would grow naturally on its own roots or to ensure that the plant grows more healthily than it would on its own roots.

herbaceous perennial - A non-woody plant that lives for two years or more, appearing from a rootstock in spring and dying down for winter.

humus - Well-rotted vegetative matter, such as leaf mould or garden compost, that bulks out the soil, increasing fertility and water retention.

hybrid - A hybrid plant occurs when two different plants are crossed, such as two species in the same genus or two species in different genera. Hybrids can occur in the wild but they are often the result of deliberate breeding to produce plants with improved characteristics to the naturally occuring forms.

informal garden - An informal garden is any garden that is not formal. Informal gardens can contain elements of formality, such as clipped hedges or straight-edged flowerbeds, but they usually lack any sort of uniformity and symmetry and are more free in their planting. Cottage gardens are generally informal.

mulch - A material used to cover bear soil to retain water and reduce weed growth. Mulches can be bark, compost, gravel, black plastic and so on.

marginal plant - Marginal plants are so named because their preferred growing conditions - moist or wet soil - are found on the margins of ponds and other water sources.

naturalize - Some plants, such as species daffodils, primroses and cyclamen, are wonderful for naturalizing, which means that they can be planted in areas where the soil is not usually cultivated, such as in grass, under trees or on banks, and allowed to spread more or less unchecked.

panorama - A wide, open view seen from one point.

parterre - A garden with formally arranged geometrical flowerbeds.

pergola - A rectangular or square garden structure consisting of an equal number of upright supports bearing long beams and a series of crossbeams. The structure creates a lightly shaded area or walkway and is often used as a support for climbing plants such as roses and clematis.

pleach - To intertwine branches, especially when making a hedge. With pleached avenues the lower branches are often also removed.

rhizome - A fleshy stem-like underground organ from which a plant can grow. Rhizomes often grow horizontally and are one of the means by which a plant spreads. Irises have rhizomes that often grow on the soil surface.

rill - A very thin stretch of water, often moving, as in a small brook. Ornamental rills, with straight, stone-line banks, are often found in formal gardens.

rootstock - This can refer to the roots of any plant but more usually is used to refer to the roots and crown of herbaceous perennials and the roots that are used in grafting.

soil pH - Some plants are very sensitive to the acidity or alkalinity of the soil, which is measured in a scale from pH1, very acid, to pH14, very alkaline; pH7 is neutral. Plants such as camellias and rhododendrons require an acid soil to grow well.

species - In each genus there is one or more species (for example *Geranium endressii*). These are individual plants that share all the same characteristics. Unlike a cultivar, a species is a distinct plant that has evolved in the wild and all its offspring look the same.

subspecies (ssp.) - These are plants within a species that vary in some way from what is regarded as the true type. They might be identical to the species but have hairier leaves, for example.

topiary - Trimming and training plants, such as box (*Buxus*) and yew (*Taxus*), into geometric and representative shapes, including orbs, spirals, pyramids, birds and animals. The trimmed plants themselves are also called topiary.

tuber - Like a bulb, a tuber is a storage organ, usually underground, from which a plant can grow. Potatoes and dahlias are tubers.

vista - In gardens, vistas are usually a view glimpsed at the end of a long narrow opening, such as an avenue of yew hedging with a statue or other focal point at the end.